BACK FROM THE BRINK

BACK FROM THE BRINK

Turning Escorts Around

Seetha

Sharad Gupta

HARPER BUSINESS

An Imprint of HarperCollins *Publishers*

First published in India in 2020 by Harper Business
An imprint of HarperCollins *Publishers*

Building 10, Tower A, 4th Floor, DLF Cyber City, Phase II,
Gurugram Haryana – 122002, India
www.harpercollins.co.in

2 4 6 8 10 9 7 5 3 1

P-ISBN: 978-93-5357-349-2
E-ISBN: 978-93-5357-350-8

Typeset in 11/16 Sabon LT Std at
Manipal Technologies Limited, Manipal

Printed and bound at
MicroPrints India, New Delhi

To the entrepreneurial spirit, which never says die

CONTENTS

FOREWORD

IT GIVES ME immense pleasure to write this foreword to the story of the Escorts legacy. Escorts is among Corporate India's highly respected companies, embodying the spirit of Indian enterprise. How H.P. Nanda built from scratch a business that he had lost during the Partition and later, in the 1980s, fought to save the group from a likely takeover is an inspiring story, as anyone who has read his memoirs, *The Days of My Years*, will know.

I knew Rajan Nanda well and we used to discuss issues relating to the economy and industry whenever we met, mostly during meetings under the Confederation of Indian Industry umbrella. He came across as a man of vision. We never spoke about our businesses, but I have learnt from this book how he has ably carried his father's legacy forward and how his son Nikhil is doing the same. A positive generational difference is there and this validates my belief in the younger generation adding value in family businesses.

Every business goes through ups and downs and some even face an existential threat. Sometimes this is because of circumstances beyond anyone's control and sometimes it is because of mistakes and wrong decisions. What is important is how the management steers the business out of the crisis. Very often, promoters are not only in denial about the troubles a company is going through but also the role their own decisions played in those troubles. Instead they tend to shift the blame on the environment, economy or the government. It is important not just to acknowledge problems but also take timely decisions to overcome them. This account sets out Escorts's own journey into troubled weather and then out of it.

A running theme in this book is about the management of change. The reforms of 1991, which brought in the much sought-after freedom for Indian businesses, also placed before them significant challenges of operating in a more competitive economy than they were used to. This book throws light on how Rajan prepared the organisation to deal with the challenges of liberalisation and also tapped into the opportunities that it opened up by steering the group into the services sector. It appears that this was partly responsible for the group's problems. There is a larger lesson to be learnt in this context. One of the mistakes Indian promoters make is over-extending businesses when the going is good, only to end up facing high debt–equity ratio. Every company should look at its special abilities and leverage these.

Nikhil appears to be dealing with a different kind of change – preparing the company for a future in which innovation and disruption will challenge long-held assumptions and business practices.

At the heart of the book is the professionalisation of a family-owned business that Rajan started and Nikhil is carrying forward to a greater degree. This is an extremely important issue. One, family members joining a business should be as well qualified as the non-family professionals. Two, it is extremely important that family-promoted businesses are run professionally so that it allows them to do well and for others working there to do better.

Escorts has always added value to the Indian economy and I am glad to note that it is continuing to do so, especially in the field of agriculture, which is so crucial to the overall economic health of the nation. Doubling farmers' income is an important initiative and a lot needs to be done on this front. Productivity improvements will have to play a big role. So will mechanisation of agriculture; more tractors need to be employed on farms. However, not all farmers can afford to own tractors. I had been thinking that there is scope for people to lease or rent out tractors in an efficient way and I am happy to know, through this book, that Escorts is playing a leading role in this.

A key message in the book is the need to focus on the consumer. Meeting consumers is very important, especially in consumer-oriented businesses and, unfortunately, not too many promoters do this. It is very important to observe consumers in the place of consumption by moving around.

I end with the hope that this book will be widely read by future managers and entrepreneurs as well as scions of business families who will inherit the business and take the family legacy forward.

I sincerely hope that they not just read this book but imbibe the lessons about how to build and grow a business as well as how to cope with crises.

Adi Godrej
Chairman, The Godrej Group

August 2019
Mumbai

PREFACE

ALL BUSINESSES ARE buffeted by numerous storms through their life. What separates the men from the boys is the way they steer themselves out of the turbulent phase. Those that emerge stronger become corporate legends; others get consigned to the scrapheap of business history.

Few, however, have faced existential threats thrice in seventy-five years. The Rs 6,000-crore engineering group Escorts Ltd, one of the icons of India Inc., has. The last crisis saw it get whittled down from an engineering group with a diversified portfolio to just three products – tractors (which accounts for 80 per cent of business), construction equipment and railway equipment. But each time it has, like the proverbial phoenix, risen again. This book tells the story of the third resurrection, when Nikhil Nanda, the third generation scion of a fabled business family, pulled Escorts back from the brink of financial ruin.

The story of Escorts actually has many layers. At one level, it is about building businesses in the face of adverse conditions.

The origins of the Faridabad-based group are small and predate India's Independence. The company started in 1944 as a trading firm, Escorts Agents, in Lahore in undivided India. Just as the company was taking wing, political developments cut it down. The Partition of India saw the founder, Hari Parshad Nanda (HPN), having to move to Delhi in much reduced pecuniary circumstances but with his fortitude and resilience intact. Slowly and painstakingly, he re-built the business. HPN soon branched out into the tractor business, first as a franchisee, then as an assembler and still later as a manufacturer.

For the next two decades Escorts expanded its portfolio to auto components, motorcycles, construction equipment and railway equipment. In the motorcycles segment, it put out two brands that took India by storm – Rajdoot and Yamaha. All this on the back of strong joint ventures with big names in each sector – Ford (tractors), Goetze and Mahle (auto components), JCB (construction equipment), Yamaha (motorcycles), Hughes Telecom (telecom equipment). Nothing but the best would do for HPN and his son Rajan Nanda. It was seen as a visionary company, generating value for its shareholders, becoming the employer of choice and contributing to national development with its array of products.

What needs to be kept in mind is that this was done in the face of a hostile policy environment – India was a controlled economy from the 1950s through the 1980s and there was government intervention at every step. Licences were required for production, there were caps on production volumes and there was price control – to name just three restrictions. Younger entrepreneurs and managers, born after 1991 when the economy was opened up, need to get a sense of that stifling environment, if only to appreciate the freedom they currently enjoy and the odds against which Escorts was built.

At another level, Escorts is a story of survival battles. In the early 1980s, there was a second near-death scare, when Escorts became the target of a corporate raid by London-based Swraj Paul. Father and son fought with their backs to the wall; they were not just up against Paul but the government of the day as well. Regulatory conditions have since changed, governments can no longer encourage such actions, but the story of that fight, detailed in H.P. Nanda's memoirs, *The Days of My Years,* is something that still holds lessons for a range of players.

Survival battles were not just fought vis-à-vis the government, but in the competitive landscape as well. The liberalisation of the economy changed the playing field of India's industrialists from the corridors of power in Delhi and state capitals to the market place. Liberalisation opened up a plethora of new opportunities and Rajan Nanda tapped into some of these. Notable ones were Escorts venturing into the healthcare and telecom space. Escorts could have become a truly diversified conglomerate, with interests in manufacturing as well as services.

But it could not manage the new competitive landscape very well, as the second, third and fourth chapters detail. They show how wrong policy decisions which ignored advice to the contrary; disconnect with customers, vendors and other stakeholders; and overcentralisation of power and authority can bring any corporate giant to its knees. Employees' salaries were delayed, air-conditioning would stop at four every evening, and banks and financial institutions refused to give it credit. Escorts had no choice but to exit several businesses, including the Escorts Heart Institute which had made it a household name across India.

Escorts was not the only pre-1991 Indian company that floundered post liberalisation. Others did too, for the same reasons as Escorts. But many of those gave up the fight, as a result of which many legendary business groups are now a pale shadow of what they once were. Indeed, they prove that oft-repeated saying: the first generation builds and grows a business, the second generation enjoys it and the third destroys it. And yet there are several exceptions to this in India; Escorts is among them. Once Rajan Nanda realised that the very existence of the group he had helped build was under threat, he accepted the need for course correction and for his son, Nikhil, to be empowered to lead that process.

This unpacks another layer of the Escorts story – that of generational change within family businesses and the tensions that this gives rise to. Unlike several other family-owned businesses, where there have been succession battles within a generation, the line of succession has been clear in Escorts. When HPN retired, the businesses were divided amicably between Rajan and his brother. Nikhil Nanda, for his part, faced no sibling claims for authority. His competition, ironically, came from his father. The chapters dealing with the crisis period and the resurrection show how different the management styles of the father and son were and how this had an adverse impact on Escorts.

The turnaround of Escorts saw Nikhil Nanda coming into his own as a manager. Assisted by a hand-picked team, he went around addressing all the pain points. The Chinese walls between departments were brought down as he knit Escorts into a cohesive organisation where everyone was aligned to a common objective – taking the company forward. Top-notch corporate talent was brought in at senior management levels and organisational goals as well as core and strategic values were codified. Financial systems and processes that had broken down were restored and reinforced. The same was done for organisational systems and processes. A new approach to industrial relations saw a balance being struck between carrots and sticks – there was too much of the former earlier. The bloated workforce was trimmed, with the help of attractive voluntary retirement and other schemes. The problem of low morale among the managerial staff was tackled through a great deal of emphasis on training and performance incentives.

Across the three businesses, customer centricity became the core around which everything else revolved. In the case of the tractors business, the focus of sales and marketing was on becoming a friend of the farmer. Not only have new products and services been launched but no opportunity is lost to connect with the customers directly. The once-broken relationship with dealers and suppliers was repaired and is being nurtured tenderly. Bridges were built with the banking and investor community. The best of consulting experience was tapped for all these and other initiatives.

All this has paid dividends. Escorts is now on a firmer financial foundation – financial year 2019 saw it record its highest ever profit after tax of Rs 484.9 crore, a 40.7 per cent increase over the previous year. It has logged the highest ever EBITDA of Rs 733.3 crore with an EBIT margin of 11.8 per cent. What is most important is that it is a more cohesive organisation. And that unpacks another layer of the Escorts story. Underlying this revival plan is Nikhil Nanda's desire to professionalise Escorts, to take it from a promoter family-driven company to one run by professionals. His father had started to give more play to professionals but had not taken it to its logical conclusion. Nikhil Nanda has, stepping back entirely from an operational role when he became chairman after his father's demise in 2018. Few Indian business families have made this transition successfully; Nikhil Nanda wants Escorts to be one of them.

With this foundation of strong finances and a professional set-up, Nikhil Nanda is preparing Escorts for the future. Innovation and disruption are now key words in the group. In September 2017, Escorts unveiled its plans to develop a compact electric tractor – the first in India. Exactly a year later, it announced that it would be launching an autonomous tractor, which will help farmers do precision-based farming. This is being done in collaboration with global technology majors. New business models are being worked on – tractor rentals and providing farmers with a range of agricultural solutions. Above all, HPN's era of strong partnerships is being revived – joint ventures with Japanese firms have been inked for tractors (with Kubota) and for construction equipment (with Tadano). The collaborations are not just about technology or giving Escorts a global footprint but also about exposing the group to a process and quality excellence culture that these companies will bring.

This book, therefore, has something for a range of readers – entrepreneurs, management executives and students, and scions of business dynasties faced with the challenge of taking their respective legacies forward. Young readers should keep two adages in mind as they read this book. One, those who do not learn from history are condemned to repeat it. Two, you have to know your history in order to learn from it.

Seetha *and* Sharad Gupta

New Delhi
August 2019

CHAPTER ONE

THE JOURNEY BEGINS[1]

ON A TYPICALLY pleasant September day in 2013, the top management of Escorts Ltd trooped into the large lunch room adjoining chairman Rajan Nanda's even bigger office and settled around the ten-seater dining table. Rajan Nanda was hosting a lunch to celebrate his son, Nikhil, being appointed managing director of the then sixty-nine-year-old engineering company. He gave a short speech about how Nikhil had it in him to lead the company.

'I am not saying it because he is my son; he has earned this position,' he said, turning a trifle emotional.

Nikhil Nanda bent down to touch his feet. As he straightened up, Rajan Nanda pulled out a ring from his pocket, took his son's hand and slipped the ring on to his finger. The gold ring with a single diamond was one which his father, H.P. Nanda, used to wear.

In placing that ring on his son's finger, Rajan Nanda was passing on the legacy of Escorts to the third generation. H.P. Nanda laid the foundation, Rajan Nanda built on it and now Nikhil Nanda had the responsibility of taking the Rs 4,000-crore company forward and steering it through ups and downs just like his grandfather and father before him.

THE UNASSUMING LOW-RISE red brick building set amidst ample greenery on the ever-busy Mathura Road in Faridabad epitomises the company it is home to – low-key and down to earth, letting its performance speak for itself. There was a brief period when this performance was nothing to write home about, but we are running ahead with the story – a story that encompasses several leaps of faith, some which worked, some which did not.

It goes back to October 1944, when two enterprising young brothers in Lahore in undivided India set up a company called Escorts Agents. Hari Parshad and Yudishter (Yudi) Nanda, born six years apart, were the sons of Bhawan Ishwar Nanda, a never-say-die businessman who had dabbled in several ventures, dusting himself off and moving on from the many setbacks he faced. His best known and longest lasting business was the Nanda Bus Service, which he started in 1930 and which networked almost the entire undivided Punjab and Kashmir, besides becoming a byword for punctuality. In building the business, Bhawan Ishwar Nanda took decisions that were considered daring – even foolish – at that time but which boosted the business.

Escorts Agents – a franchise for domestic electrical appliances of the American white goods company Westinghouse – was really Yudi's baby. Looking as he was to branching out on his own, he was quick to realise the potential of the franchise when he was offered it. The elite were craving high-end gadgets, and Escorts Agents could help meet that demand. The name Escorts came from the idea of the company, in a sense, escorting the goods to customers. A doting elder brother, Hari Parshad (HPN), who was managing the bus operations, arranged money for the business.

Yudi's gut feeling had been right – the business quickly expanded to other cities in undivided Punjab. But barely three years later, it fell prey to circumstances beyond anyone's control – the Partition of

India in 1947. A large consignment of goods it had imported from Westinghouse arrived in Lahore when the Nandas had moved to India. There was no way to access those goods and Escorts Agents lost all the money it had invested in them.

This was far, far worse than any of the reverses their father had suffered, but HPN and Yudi proved they had inherited his indomitable spirit. Displaying ample chutzpah and relying on the goodwill that the Nanda Bus Service had earned in what was now two sides of an international border, the brothers went about rebuilding their business.

Two things brought them that goodwill. One, the Nanda Bus Service and Escorts Agents had never defaulted on their loan repayments to the National Bank of India (now ANZ Grindlays). Because of this track record, the bank unhesitatingly gave them a Rs 1 lakh loan to resume business, even though there was Rs 4 lakh outstanding credit. Incidentally, HPN later repaid all his debts in Pakistan, even though the Indian government had passed exemption orders. Two, the Nanda Bus Service had provided trucks and buses on credit to the Indian National Congress during the 1945 provincial elections in Punjab. The Congress could repay only half of the Rs 10 lakh it owed Nanda Bus Service when Partition happened. Senior Congress leaders had signed promissory notes in favour of the company.

The finance gave the initial momentum and Escorts Agents resumed operations in 1948. HPN and Yudi both believed that spending money will bring in more money and that appearances matter. So they invested in a two-room office in Connaught Place in Delhi and did it up quite elaborately, causing much consternation among the other partners. One of them, ironically, was Vittal Mallya (the founder of India's leading liquor company United Breweries), whose own son, Vijay, came to epitomise showy extravagance close to sixty years later.

But that was typical of the Nanda brothers. Though he had come to Delhi with just Rs 5,000 and two cars, HPN put up his wife and two elder children at the tony Imperial Hotel. 'I could scarce afford it but I felt that by maintaining a certain standard of living, I could pick up the threads with my old business acquaintances,' he wrote in his memoirs. He explained the fancy office interiors in a similar vein: 'We felt a good-looking office was important to our corporate image.'

The slow rebuilding of the business got underway. Escorts Agents went back to Westinghouse, but this time for franchise of power generation equipment as well. A large contract put out by the Punjab government was up for grabs and the Nanda brothers made a bold pitch for it. But the Westinghouse–Escorts Agents combine was up against two big players – English Electric from the United Kingdom and General Electric (GE) from the United States. When, despite its best efforts, the combine's pitch was $1.5 million costlier than that of GE, HPN decided to tap into his vast array of contacts in the Congress party. Many remembered how the Nanda Bus Service had helped – both in undivided Punjab and later during Partition – and this swung the contract for Escorts Agents in 1951. HPN tore up the old promissory notes that could have got him Rs 5 lakh – a big sum in those early days – once again earning him the eternal gratitude of the Congress bigwigs.

HPN demonstrated repeatedly through his career that businesses cannot be built sitting in closed rooms and behind ornate desks alone; that it was equally important to forge and sustain relationships across an entire spectrum of people – big, not-so-big and small. His tall, well-dressed frame and handsome looks were enhanced by the charm that he exuded. A quintessential people's man, he could call up a chief minister and invite him for a lunch of rajma chawal at the Escorts factory in Faridabad, tell a Union finance minister that he was coming over for coffee, hobnob with global business leaders and be chummy with factory workers, dancing the bhangra with one and asking another to recite Urdu couplets.

As a result, not only did he build up a vast network of friends, acquaintances and well-wishers who would rally around whenever he was in trouble, this constant interaction also helped him gauge what there could be a market for. When, as a vexed child, Nikhil asked his grandfather why the newspaper was more interesting than spending time with a grandson back home on school vacation, HPN said: 'The newspapers tell me what the country needs and what I can provide.'

Did his decision to set up Escorts Agricultural Machines Limited (EAM) in 1948 stem from some such realisation that this was what the country's farmers needed? That is not clear; all he says in his memoirs is that he was getting bored with the transport business (the Nanda Bus Service had been continued and HPN had used its old reputation and his many contacts to get route permits for buses and trucks) and he wanted to start off on his own. But this decision – EAM started by taking up the franchise for farm equipment and tractors of American company Minneapolis Moline – would make him eventually a crusader for farm mechanisation in the country.

'I WANT TO bring the world's best to India and take India's best to the world,' HPN had told a teenage Nikhil when asked what his ambition was. This was in the late 1980s, but that had been the motto that drove HPN from the very beginning. India was just a fledgling country when he started out and he could hardly offer India's best at that time, so he concentrated on getting the world's best to India.

In 1949, British company Ferguson brought thirty new tractors to India for a demonstration. HPN started out by wanting to crush the competition on his turf; instead he got sold on the state-of-the-art tractors, which he found more suited to Indian conditions. Barely a year into EAM's Minneapolis Moline franchise, he lost no time in switching dealerships. The decision was made easier by the fact that the Minneapolis Moline tractors had become uncompetitive because of the devaluation of the rupee vis-à-vis the dollar.

Bringing the world's best to India, for HPN, was not just about importing world-class equipment, whether power equipment or tractors; it was forging partnerships that would build up India's capability to offer its best to the world. What better way to do this than to get one's hands dirty with manufacturing and what better way to learn this than by partnering with global leaders?

The first foray into manufacturing was not with tractors, though. It was to manufacture piston rings with technology from German company Goetze. Goetze India was incorporated in 1954. By this time, Escorts Agents and EAM had merged into one company, Escorts Ltd, after Yudi's tragic death in a plane crash in 1952. Over time, more such tie-ups with German companies were to be forged, changing Escorts' profile from a trading and marketing company to an engineering company.

The tractor manufacturing business had far more modest origins, in comparison. The impetus was, however, similar – it was not enough to keep importing and distributing; a road map for manufacturing was also needed. So, in 1950, Escorts started importing Ferguson tractors in semi-knocked-down condition and assembled them in a workshop on Delhi's Roshanara Road. But it was a feeling of betrayal that provided the impetus for Escorts to take the first big step towards becoming India's largest tractor manufacturer for nearly thirty years.

In 1953, Canadian company Massey Harris bought up Ferguson, giving birth to Massey Ferguson. That move was soon to give Escorts its first big shock. The new company bought an engine manufacturing plant in the United Kingdom, the franchise for which was held by Simpson India, a part of the Amalgamations group. It then set up a joint venture company with the Amalgamations group, called Tractors and Farm Equipment (TAFE) Limited. It then also reneged on a deal HPN had with the Amalgamations group founder, S. Anantharamakrishnan, on how Escorts and Amalgamations were to split the tractors being imported to India. Escorts had, by then, built up a network of dealers and mechanics, besides a training school, all of which were now in danger. Finally, when he came to know that Massey Ferguson had started poaching Escorts dealers, a furious HPN vowed to beat it at its own game. 'After having spent years establishing the Ferguson tractors, I was now out to undo it all,' he wrote in his memoirs.

How he went about it showed the pugnacious side of HPN – he could give back as good as he got, something a certain London-based Indian tycoon was to realise three decades later.

First, he started importing tractors from a Yugoslav licensee of Massey Ferguson and adroitly checkmated the latter's move to block this competition from its own stable. Then he learnt that 200 tractors manufactured by Polish firm URSUS were languishing in Indian ports. URSUS was not exactly the world's best, but HPN realised this offered him a window of opportunity. Putting aside his ego, he reached out to Roland Heath, who had been instrumental in the initial partnership with Ferguson and with whom he had a falling out later, and convinced him to help Escorts develop a tractor, using these URSUS tractors as a base.

The Third Five Year Plan (1961–66) made import substitution and indigenisation policy goals, mainly because of constraints on foreign exchange. The tractors that Heath helped develop – Escort 37 and Escort 27 – had 50 per cent indigenous components, and Escorts applied for a licence to manufacture these in collaboration with URSUS. The government first gave permission for Escorts to import CKD kits (completely knocked down kits of non-assembled parts) from Poland.

In the late 1960s, the first Escorts tractor rolled off the assembly line at the factory in Faridabad. The Escorts tryst with Faridabad had started with a factory making X-ray equipment in collaboration with Westinghouse. Over the years, the fate of the company and the town were to get intertwined inextricably, as Escorts forayed into motorcycles, construction equipment and railway equipment, even as it continued its partnerships with German companies on automobile components.

The desire to get the world's best to India was still there. So was the resolve to outsell Massey Ferguson. A way to do both would soon present itself.

In 1968, the government decided to hand out more tractor manufacturing licences because it realised the country needed more tractors. With seven years' manufacturing experience under its belt, Escorts formed a joint venture with Ford Motor Company of the United States to manufacture its 47 HP (horsepower) tractor. The joint venture was housed in a new company, Escorts Tractors Limited.

HPN admits in his memoirs that, globally, Massey Ferguson was a greater success than Ford at that time. 'I was dying to get my teeth into this new challenge and reverse the order.' He achieved that. Soon, Ford was outselling Massey Ferguson in India. Well into the late 1980s, there were long waiting lists for Ford tractors which stretched to over a year. One customer tried getting a recommendation letter from Devi Lal, then deputy prime minister. Lal was the patriarch of one of the three powerful political dynasties in Haryana and needed to be accommodated. The customer moved up the list, but still had to wait a few months.

There were other partnerships – with British company J.C. Bamford Excavators Limited (JCB) for construction equipment in

1979, with Yamaha Motor Company for motorcycles (Escorts was already manufacturing the iconic Rajdoot motorcycles with Polish technology) and with German firm Claas to manufacture harvester combines. How Escorts got into the construction equipment business is both an example of HPN's ingenuity and the policy environment that businesses had to operate in those days. Apart from licensing (with licences setting limits on quantum of production), price controls had become common across many sectors. When prices of tractors were capped in the early 1970s, it dealt a huge blow to the industry. Escorts decided to start manufacturing construction equipment, which were out of the price control regime. These were, HPN explains in his memoirs, basically tractors with add-ons, but the change in nomenclature helped Escorts price them without any interference.

HPN WAS NOT just forging partnerships and growing the business; he was also building an institution, putting in place systems and processes that were often a first for Indian businesses.

If Ferguson's demo tractors impressed HPN so much that he wanted to become a franchisee, the British company was equally impressed with the quality of service that Escorts provided for the Minneapolis Moline tractors which it was selling. Every customer was given vouchers for six free services – on the farm. Moreover, the final price for the customer was the same, irrespective of location. This was to prevent dealers from using local taxes as an excuse to raise prices. Other manufacturers followed the Escorts example.

But this pales in comparison to one lasting contribution that Escorts made to the tractor industry – an institute of farm mechanisation. In a country predominantly using bullock-drawn ploughs in those days, he realised that unless farmers and operators were trained in using tractors, they would end up damaging them. That would be lose-lose all around. Farmers would not have faith in tractors, the reputation of tractor manufacturers would be hit (since the blame would be assigned to the tractor) and the country's farm mechanisation process would simply stall.

A training school was first set up in the Azadpur locality of Delhi in 1951 but was later moved out to Kashipur in Uttar Pradesh. Farmers and students got both theoretical and practical training. In 1969, the institute moved to Bangalore where, as the Escorts Training and Development Centre (the name it got in 2012), it trains not just farmers and mechanics from India but also from countries in Europe and Asia where Escorts tractors are exported to. The Karnataka State Agro-Industrial Corporation has often sent its officials for training programmes at ETDC. Spread over 90 acres, the centre is equipped not just with tractors but also workshops and a centralised nursery, among other things. All engineer trainees in Escorts, including those in the construction equipment division, spend at least a month at the centre. So do the sales and marketing executives who are brought up to date on new products and the USP of Escorts products, especially vis-à-vis competition. The training for farmers and mechanics is also customised to suit individuals – trainers identify gaps in learners' skills and plug those during the training.

Later, in the mid-1970s, two other path-breaking initiatives were taken, both stemming from enlightened self-interest.

The first was the Escorts Employees Ancillaries Limited (EEAL), which was owned and run by the employees along with Escorts, which had a 30 per cent stake in the company. The units set up by EEAL supplied components to Escorts, which helped them with pre-feasibility studies, as well as technical collaborations. A company on similar lines, Alpha Toyo, was started for the wives of Escorts executives a year later.

HPN writes that he was killing two birds with one stone with what he describes as a 'historic venture in industrial democracy'. For one, this provided assured supply lines for crucial components; in those days a large number of items were reserved for production only in the small-scale sector (the capital investment ceiling was a measly Rs 10 lakh in the 1970s) and so Escorts was not allowed to manufacture them. Secondly, this also helped stave off any political interference in the company's management. During the Emergency period (1975–77), Prime Minister Indira Gandhi's younger son, Sanjay, was making noises about having labour representatives on the boards of companies. With this masterstroke, HPN could claim to be already involving employees in management. In 2001, EEAL, which was supplying carburettors, oil pumps and clutches mainly for the two-wheelers Escorts manufactured, was renamed as Escorts Auto Components Ltd.[2]

And then there was EDDAL (Escorts Dealer Development Association Ltd), something no tractor manufacturer has to date. The brainchild of Madan Agarwal, who headed the tractor operations for many years, EDDAL is a kind of a cooperative of dealers, with the objective of helping each other. Dealers – the first point of contact for customers – can make or break any automobile company. Keeping dealers up to date, well financed and motivated is, therefore, important and this is what EDDAL was set up to do.

The cooperative model was to knit them into a family, where each member helps the other. Dealers pay a certain sum from the sale of every tractor (and motorcycle when Escort was selling Rajdoot and Yamaha bikes), with Escorts also chipping in. The interest this corpus earned is ploughed back into EDDAL, the majority of directors of which are dealers. Using this money, EDDAL trains dealers, helps them set up their business and gives them loans on easy instalments.

BY THE 1980s, Escorts was among the bluest of the blue chips in Corporate India, with a presence in several sectors (making tractors, two wheelers, auto components, construction equipment, railway equipment) delivering value for the shareholders (it had gone public in 1960 and was oversubscribed sixteen times then), and was the first choice for job-seeking youth from both the prestigious IITs (Indian Institute of Technology) and ITIs (Industrial Training Institute). Rohtash Mal, who was CEO of the tractor division of Escorts from 2006 to 2012, recalls standing in a queue of over 100 people to pick up application forms for the company's graduate engineer trainee programme when he passed out of IIT in 1976. In the middle class localities of Faridabad, any young man with a job in Escorts was flooded with matrimonial offers and was assured of a big, fat dowry as well. The top management consisted of highly respected professionals and the board of directors was packed with stellar names.

But soon all that was going to be threatened as Escorts faced its second near-death challenge.

In 1983, Escorts, along with another highly respected Delhi company, DCM, founded by Lala Shri Ram, fell prey to a corporate raid. London-based Indian businessman Swraj Paul started buying up shares of both companies stealthily with what clearly was an attempt to take them over, exploiting loopholes in rules relating to investments by non-resident Indians (NRIs).

HPN's fighting spirit resurfaced with renewed vigour. In 1947, he and Yudi had to rebuild what they had lost. In 1953, when he decided to teach Massey Ferguson a lesson for betraying him, he stood to lose just one part of the business empire he was putting in place. This time everything he had built up over three decades was at stake. '*Jab marna hai, to kya nahin karna hai* (When death is staring you in the face, don't stop at anything),' was one of his favourite phrases. If all this was going to be taken away, he was going to fight to his last breath.

It was an unequal battle, however. Paul very clearly had the backing of the government of the day, led by Mrs Indira Gandhi. Escorts was squeezed in multiple ways; attempts were made to scare away other industrialists who showed solidarity; there were raids at the home of HPN's elder son, Rajan. A protracted legal battle saw Escorts getting a favourable judgement in the Bombay High Court which was reversed in the Supreme Court. The historic battle – a never-to-be-forgotten chapter in Indian corporate history – ended only after an out-of-court settlement following a change in government, with Rajiv Gandhi becoming prime minister.

It had been a harrowing time for Escorts; the top management's attention was diverted to this battle; its various projects and proposals were blocked (the licence-permit-quota raj was very much in place then). During this crisis, once again the strength of HPN's contacts became evident. Though some industrialists distanced themselves from him, others helped him quietly while Escorts shareholders rallied behind the company, as did the dealers.

HPN managed to save his beloved empire, but the fight had drained him. Daughter-in-law Ritu recalls that he was a completely changed man after that. He was in his late sixties then and he decided to slowly step back and let his sons, Rajan and Anil, take more and more responsibility for day-to-day operations though it would be another ten years before he formally handed over the baton to Rajan. Both sons had joined Escorts while in their late teens. Both had been put through internships with Escorts partners – Rajan to MAN (Maschinenfabrik Augsburg Nurnberg) in Germany as well as Lucas and Grindlays in the United Kingdom and Anil to Ford in the United States and Goetze and Mahle in Germany. HPN started spending less time at the Escorts corporate office on Kasturba Gandhi

Marg in Delhi, from where he used to largely operate. The corporate office shifted to Faridabad in the mid-1990s, but the Delhi office, located at the junction of Kasturba Gandhi Marg and the outer circle of Connaught Place, continued to remain a landmark for Delhiites till 2016.

HPN's last major contribution to the Escorts empire was perhaps the Escorts Heart Institute and Research Centre – the first such specialised institution in the private sector in India and the first hospital run on corporate lines (large business houses had set up hospitals earlier, but they were in the nature of philanthropy). This was again HPN's vision and yearning to use business to address some unmet need of the country at work. As will be detailed elsewhere in the book, EHIRC set new standards not just in cardiac surgery and treatment but in the way hospitals were run and provided care.

Generational shift was not the only change Escorts saw. In 1991, Prime Minister P.V. Narasimha Rao and Finance Minister Manmohan Singh liberalised the Indian economy. Licences were passé, businessmen didn't have to run to the government for sundry permissions any more. But competition also increased and became cut-throat. Suddenly the old ways of doing business were not relevant any more. Perhaps HPN began to realise this. Though he had always railed against the stifling socialism that Indian businesses had laboured under (he was a member of the Forum for Free Enterprise and even fought an election on the Swatantra Party – the only party that openly spoke for free markets – ticket), he had always operated in that closed scenario. The new playing ground had different rules of the game. It was time to formally let go.

CHAPTER TWO

FASHIONING A NEW ESCORTS

ON 31 MARCH 1994, as members of the board of directors of Escorts Ltd trooped into the Versailles-La Rochelle restaurant at the Oberoi Intercontinental hotel in Delhi[1], they were only expecting to discuss the items on the agenda. Little did they know that in that golden jubilee year of Escorts, the board meeting would see the end of one era and birth of a new one.

Soon after the proceedings got under way, Chairman and Managing Director H.P. Nanda announced he was stepping down and handing over charge to his two sons, Rajan, who was then Vice-Chairman and Managing Director, and Anil, Managing Director. Rajan was to be Chairman of the Escorts Group and Anil the Vice-Chairman.

The stunned directors – among them legendary technocrat Mantosh Sondhi, top industrialists Dr Parvinder Singh of Ranbaxy and Arun Bharat Ram of DCM, former Reserve Bank of India governor M. Narasimham and noted physicist M.G.K. Menon – refused to agree but when HPN insisted, the meeting was suspended for a while. Sondhi came out of the hall and broke the news to top management executives waiting outside. 'We have asked for time to digest this; we will return and ask him to reconsider,' he told the equally shocked executives.

HPN, however, would not reconsider. He was getting on in years, he pointed out, and his sons had proved themselves to be excellent managers eminently capable of taking the company forward, adding that he would rather have the division happen amicably while he was alive than with a lot of bickering and acrimony later, as had happened in other business families. The board insisted he continue as Chairman Emeritus and Founder Advisor, to which he agreed. He had one request – that the management information reports be sent to him, which they were. He would read reports at home and, occasionally, ring up if he was worried about a particular issue. Beyond that, he kept his distance from the business.

HPN was seventy-seven years old and he was feeling weary; the corporate battle with Swraj Paul had drained him and the death of his wife, Raj, in 1990 had been a blow. He had gradually started leaving more and more work to Rajan and Anil; he realised and accepted that the new liberalised business environment that the 1991 economic reforms had ushered in was something they would be better off handling.

'At a time when the country as well as the Escorts Group of Companies are entering into a new era of globalisation and economic growth, it is only prudent to usher in a new stewardship of management,' he wrote in a letter to business partners in October that year, informing them of the changes.

THE SHIFT WAS not just generational; it was also going to herald a new management style. Rajan Nanda was like his father in many ways – tall and handsome, with a taste for dressing well and a life that revolved around Escorts. He had joined the business in his late teens, after deciding that academics was not his cup of tea after just a year in college. After watching from the sidelines for a while, he started off as a purchase manager in 1963, when he was just twenty-one. Two years later, he was made plant manager of Plant 1, the tractor factory. He would spend long hours in the office – often being the first to come in at 8 a.m. – and family holidays too were planned around business trips. 'I just took to business like a duck to water,' he had told Dilip Bobb of *India Today* in an interview in the early 1980s.[2]

At the time Rajan Nanda took over from his father, Escorts was a blue-chip stock, trading at around Rs 80 a share. Escorts may have been synonymous with HPN, but Rajan Nanda's own contribution to its growth was not insignificant. As HPN identified new business opportunities, strategised and negotiated a policy environment that was becoming increasingly restrictive, operating mostly out of the Kasturba Gandhi Marg office, Rajan Nanda immersed himself in operations in Faridabad and was closely involved in the setting up of the factories of the Escorts group. Old-timers at Escorts recall his keen grasp of issues and ability to get to the bottom of things, as a result of which far more professionally qualified engineers and managers found it near impossible to run circles around him. There is little dispute about his role in the tractor division becoming profitable – for the first time in 1975 – and remaining so ever since; he had gone into every aspect of operations, bringing in economies of scale and improving processes.

Rajan Nanda stayed away from close involvement in the businesses that his brother, Anil, was in charge of – the auto components and two-wheeler business. HPN was more involved in those and the motor scooter division rolled out motorcycles that would be the rage among the youth in the 1970s and '80s. One of them was the Rajdoot GTS that came to be known as the Bobby bike after featuring in the

’70s teenage romance film *Bobby*. The more macho Yamaha Rajdoot 350 was promoted in another teenage romance a decade later, *Hero*. This bike also came to be known as Yamdoot (a combination of Yamaha and Rajdoot), the messenger of the god of death, Yama.

Rajan Nanda also shared his father’s belief in partnering with the world’s best. He had been instrumental in procuring technology for pick-and-carry cranes for the construction equipment division from New Zealand in 1971 and this had put Escorts among the major global producers. HPN had identified Ford as a partner for tractors in the 1960s, but Rajan Nanda had played a key role in the negotiations; wife Ritu recalls that their honeymoon in 1969 was all about that joint venture. Many of the later joint ventures Escorts got into – with Britain’s J.C. Bamford Excavators (JCB) in 1979, Germany’s farm equipment firm Claas in 1989 and American telecom company Hughes Network Systems in 1991, to name just three – were Rajan Nanda’s initiatives.

So was the sprawling Escorts Research and Development Centre that came up in 1977. Headed by M.M. Mehta, whom HPN had ardently wooed out of G.B. Pant Agricultural University, this went much beyond the R&D efforts that were needed in order to meet the stringent indigenisation norms in place at that time, thanks mainly to Rajan Nanda’s constant encouragement. As will be seen later, this centre in its later avatar as Knowledge Management Centre became the fulcrum of innovation in the company.

Though Rajan Nanda held HPN in very high esteem (apart, of course, from the very loving father–son relationship they shared), he did not wait for permission or even consultation before every move. He had his own mind and convictions and, when given a responsibility, he would go out and do what it took to fulfil it. Father and son would clash often, though privately HPN would take pride in Rajan Nanda's achievements (a story that was to play out between him and his son, Nikhil, a couple of decades later). So when Rajan Nanda took over as chairman, he was very clear about how he wanted to proceed.

'OUR GOLDEN JUBILEE heralds the genesis of a new Escorts. The Escorts for the new India, the new world.' With these words Rajan Nanda signed off his first Chairman's Statement in the annual report of 1993-94.

The new Escorts was going to be structured very differently from what it had been till then. The group had undoubtedly achieved a formidable position in the Indian corporate landscape, but the growth over the previous fifty years had been a tad unstructured and unplanned. As a result, the multiple sectors it was in were being handled by multiple divisions, with often overlapping functions. In two-wheelers, tractors and construction equipment, there were two entities each – an Escorts entity and a joint venture. In case of tractors, there was a tractor division in Escorts Ltd that handled the manufacturing operations; a farm equipment division that handled the marketing; and an Escorts Research Centre in the corporate office that provided the designs. Each of these was a separate profit centre, with a system of transfer pricing between them and each was headed by powerful managers fiercely protective of their individual turfs. The farm equipment division purchased tractors from the tractor division as well as from Escorts Tractors Ltd (the joint venture with Ford), and sold both to the market. With competition increasing all around, there was recognition of the need to identify areas where Escorts could be competitive and strengthen them. Rajan Nanda had set up a strategic planning department in the corporate office and brought in a thirty-something Rajan Swaroop to head it.

A few weeks before the 31 March board meeting, an internal circular signed by both Rajan and Anil Nanda outlined a restructuring plan for Escorts Ltd (the leadership changeover came into effect retrospectively from 4 March). 'With change in the countrys economic scenario, and the intensely competitive markets in which we have to perform, it has become essential to restructure the organisation by combing its strengths, to make a more independent business model that can work autonomously to integrate Management, Products and Markets [sic],' the circular said.

Consequently, similar businesses were grouped together for focussed attention from the corporate centre. Six such business verticals were set up:

- An Engineering Products Division had Escorts Herion, the Railway Equipment Division and Auto Suspension Parts under its supervision.
- The Farm Machinery Division combined the tractors manufacturing and marketing functions.
- An Automotive Components Division was in charge of the Automotive Division (AMD) and Goetze India.
- A Construction Machinery business oversaw the Escorts JCB joint venture as well as the Industrial Equipment Division (IED, the construction equipment division of Escorts Ltd). A wholly owned subsidiary, Escorts Construction Equipment Ltd, was incorporated and took over the business of IED in 1995.
- A Two Wheeler business was given responsibility for MSD, Yamaha Motorcycle Division and EEAL. A year later, these, too, were brought under a new wholly owned subsidiary, Escorts Automotives Ltd. In addition, a 50:50 joint venture between Escorts and Yamaha Motor Company Ltd was incorporated,

into which Escorts Automotives spun off the Yamaha Motorcycle Division in 1996.

- The Telecommunication Division, which was producing EPABX systems, was the only one left untouched at that point because the company was in talks with a foreign partner for a collaboration. Later that year, a wholly owned subsidiary, Escorts Communication, was set up to take over this business.

Each business had a chief executive officer (CEO), responsible and accountable for all aspects of performance, from operations to market performance and profits. The proposed changes, the circular said, would put all the resources of the company at the command of the business heads, enabling them to build successful business enterprises. However, while the businesses were independent in almost every respect, central reporting through some corporate departments like finance, human resource management, law and strategic planning continued.

There was also acknowledgement that merely re-jigging departments with the same people would be pointless, that new systems would need new people. Rajan Nanda went about appointing younger, professional talent, 'with an international perspective', as he wrote in the 1993-94 annual report. A board of management was also set up, made up of CEOs of individual businesses and key corporate functionaries; this was to interact closely with the board of directors which was to set the overall direction.

For Rajan Nanda, this was an important step, as what he said in two interviews around twenty years apart shows. 'I am a hardliner on professional management ... My contribution is to make Escorts a business-management-oriented industry and my main objective is to institutionalise the business,' he had told Bobb. In 2003, in a television programme, *Face to Face,* he told host Karan Thapar,

'When I stepped in I realised I had to convert an individual-led company into an institution, so I became a very professionally oriented man.' That did not quite happen, however, as the future trajectory of Escorts will show, but that had more to do with his personal style rather than lack of intention.

The sharper business focus this restructuring brought about showed initial signs of success. The Escorts Group income in 1994-95 saw a 34.7 per cent increase over 1993-94; importantly, profits surged 334 per cent over the previous year. Every group company contributed to this.

The restructuring exercise was also about Rajan Nanda building his own team. He had an uneasy equation with the older executives of his father's time. They were highly qualified professionals (something he acknowledged and respected), but they tended to patronise him, perhaps because they had seen him from the time he was a little child, and this irked him. 'I had to prove myself to the senior people who thought I was impulsive and rash. I have been criticised all the way but I realised you have to handle today in the context of tomorrow,' he admitted to Bobb.

HPN also often found himself caught between his contemporaries and his son. Though he did not quite approve of his son's style of functioning, he never encouraged the seniors, who reported to him, to undercut Rajan. He would tell them to keep Rajan informed about key developments. Rajan perhaps realised this and so coped with the ancien regime as best as he could as long as his father was still in the saddle, waiting for them to retire or move out on their own. By the time he became chairman, not many of them remained, and he moved his chosen people into key positions. All of them were in their forties and so were others who were appointed later. Two people became his closest confidants and advisers. One was Umesh Banerji, the soft-spoken chief financial officer (CFO), who was the same age as Rajan and had been with Escorts since 1974. He was among the very few who never shied away from speaking the truth to Rajan. The other was forty-three-year-old Rakesh Chopra, who had joined Escorts in the late '80s and had been deputed to Escorts–JCB when there was a vacuum there. Rajan brought him back in 1994 to head the farm equipment division and he went on to become the longest-serving CEO of that business.

RAJAN NANDA AND his new team had their work cut out for them. The 1991 liberalisation meant businesses could now breathe free – they no longer had to run to the government for licences and permissions, whether on production or prices – but it also brought with it increased competition, not just domestic but from foreign shores as well. Many joint ventures that Indian companies had with global majors at that time were unions of compulsion; foreign companies had not been allowed to set up wholly owned subsidiaries and they had to partner with an Indian company. With that restriction being lifted gradually, sector by sector, there was a rash of corporate divorces from the mid-1990s; some foreign companies sought to walk away from existing joint ventures and set up new greenfield ventures, others sought to buy out their Indian partners.

Escorts could not remain unaffected, and the tractor division was the first to face this challenge.

Over the twenty-odd years since the joint venture with Ford was inked, the American company had bought another farm equipment company called New Holland and then, in the early '90s, sold Ford New Holland to Fiat Geotech, which now decided to unite all the different farm equipment brands under one New Holland brand. As a result, the joint venture partner in Escorts Tractor Ltd was now New Holland. Soon after Rajan Nanda became chairman, New Holland approached Escorts, asking it to flip the shareholding pattern; it now wanted to become the majority partner with a 60 per cent stake. Escorts refused and said it would buy out New Holland's 40 per cent stake instead. After protracted negotiations led by Rajan Nanda and Chopra, the joint venture was dissolved and Escorts Tractor Ltd got merged with Escorts.

Escorts also bargained for and got a one-year window to change the brand. In the event, it did not need one year; it had started work on a new name even as negotiations for ending the partnership were on and, within a couple of months of the formal separation, it was ready to start selling with a new name – Farmtrac. Finding a name was the easier part. Far more challenging would be transferring the formidable brand equity of Ford – stories are legion about farmers queuing up outside the factory gates to buy it – to Farmtrac. In doing this, there were external and internal challenges that had to be dealt with.

The biggest was increased competition. Escorts had been the leader in the tractor market till the late '80s. Several players emerged and faded away but its main competitors had been TAFE and Mahindra Tractors (both of which had also started operations in the '60s) and, to a lesser extent, VST Tillers, which started producing tractors in 1982. From the mid-'90s, however, not only were there more domestic players, but big global names also made their India presence more than felt.

By this time, Escorts had already lost its market leader position to Mahindra. In 1990, Mahindra accounted for 31 per cent of the market, TAFE 29 per cent and Escorts 25 per cent. It had not happened overnight, but over a period of a few years – a period when

Escorts became complacent and its rivals stole a march over it by improving their products and aggressively marketing the changes. Escorts already had some of these features but had not played them up. Apart from this, it had also come out with a new series of tractors in the early '90s which, dealers of that time recall, customers rejected outright, forcing the series to be withdrawn. This also exposed the lack of coordination between the operations and R&D departments and the marketing department. It was clear that Escorts needed to fix a lot of things within the organisation.

This got underscored when, soon after he had taken charge, Chopra had a chance encounter with a senior executive of a consulting firm at a relative's wedding. His advice to Chopra was succinct: wake up and smell the coffee that your competitors are brewing. Some digging around showed that one firm had been closely working with the consulting firm on improving practically every process and had not stinted on money.

The Escorts plants, on the other hand, were just not geared for the requirements of a highly competitive market. Not only was the technology obsolete – the Polish technology was still being used – but the factories were also inefficient and overstaffed. Internal processes, especially those relating to quality, were weak. And there was debilitating internal politics. With little time to lose, Chopra hired a British consulting firm to completely re-engineer the plants.

The business process re-engineering (BPR) exercise started in 1996 in Plant 1, where the Escorts brand of tractors were produced. A nine-member cross-functional team of people in their late twenties and thirties (only one person was around fifty years old) was put in place. The team sat in a glass cabin on the shop floor and workers were free to come in and interact with them and understand what they were doing; the idea was to win trust through transparency. Earlier the plant was organised on functional lines, with heads of materials, supply chain, production and quality reporting to a plant head. Since they were responsible for their individual jurisdictions and not the final product, each would pass the buck to another whenever there was a problem. Chopra's brief to the team was simple – take two or three years but transform this completely.

That is what was done over the next three years. Functional heads gave way to product heads. So, one person was in charge of and accountable for, say, engines – right from sourcing materials to final quality. There was now little scope to shift the blame to some other department. Heads of different product units reported to the plant head. The plant layout was also changed from a process-oriented one to a product-focussed one. This meant that all processes required for, say, the engine were grouped together into one cohesive engine unit and those required for transmission were grouped together into one cohesive transmission unit.

But the bold move had almost got scuppered in the first year itself, soon after the layout was drawn up. The need arose for new engine assembly and testing facilities and that would have meant an investment of around Rs 35-40 crore for just one plant. When the proposal was moved at the corporate office, one senior executive questioned its need – a query that Rajan Nanda bounced to Chopra. Chopra went back and told the BPR team to work on justifying the investment.

The team started to do so. As luck would have it, Rajan Nanda planned to come around for a plant visit one day. When Chopra got wind of it, he told the team head, Shailendra Agrawal, to put up the drawing of the layout on a board and be prepared for a thorough grilling. He knew it would pique Rajan Nanda's interest. Sure enough, the chairman came, saw and asked questions. When they were answered to his satisfaction, he said, 'Oh, very good, please go ahead.' Now with the chairman's backing, the BPR exercise went ahead in full steam.

It was not easy to implement, though. The exercise was challenging the prevailing organisational structure, driving the point that specialisation beyond a point would prove counter-productive and that everyone should be prepared to do any kind of work. Naturally, then, there was resistance, from both the managerial staff and the workers. The functional heads saw it as a clipping of their wings, which, perhaps, it was – this was the only way to painlessly take people who were not in tune with modern practices out of positions where they could impede progress. In a way, this exercise replicated the top-level management changes, where younger people were given bigger roles. In the plants, the managers often saw the reassignment of responsibilities from functional to product basis as a demotion; someone who had always been with supplies resented reporting to someone who had been handling production and vice versa. But with the top management backing the initiative, everyone had to come around. Chopra would often visit the shop floor and spend a couple of hours with the BPR team. That sent out a powerful message, apart from boosting their morale.

The BPR exercise soon covered other plants of the farm equipment division, including the erstwhile Ford plant (which was now Plant 2). The construction equipment plant had started the BPR around the same time as the farm equipment division, but it was not as successful. For the farm equipment division, though, this was a turning point. It got a modern plant, with the latest technology and processes; close to Rs 250 crore was spent on getting, among other things, the latest torque control and the best Japanese paint shop. New collaborations were inked – a joint venture with Italian firm Carraro for axles and transmissions and a longer-term technological partnership with Austrian firm AVL for a new series of engines. The exercise set a target of a 60-80 per cent improvement in productivity, quality, cost and inventory management and managed to achieve all this. The capacity of the plants in Faridabad increased from less than 56,250 tractors to 72,000, enabling the company to defer plans to set up a new plant in Ranjangaon in Maharashtra. Importantly, managers became more cross-functional than before. It gave Escorts a solid foundation, which helped it cope with some very stormy weather that was soon to set in.

There were other initiatives as well. Chopra hired leading consulting firms to reduce material and manpower costs and to work out a marketing strategy. The Escorts tractor was re-branded as Powertrac, a new series of tractors in the 30-35 HP range was introduced – which not only helped fill a gap in Escorts product portfolio but the performance of which was also much better because of improved engines and transmission – and a 40 HP tractor under the Farmtrac brand was launched. All this notwithstanding, the company's market share kept slipping.

Work also began on designing a tractor for south India. The latter was much needed. For long, Escorts had not looked beyond the northern markets, which accounted for over 60 per cent of the tractor market. But when the northern market got saturated, it did not have a product or strategy for the south, where demand was picking up. The hard soil and wet land operations of the south required a different tractor from what was used for the alluvial soil of the north. Rivals TAFE and Mahindra had got suitable tractors; Escorts did not. Unfortunately, Escorts did not make much headway in designing a tractor for the south and, twenty years later, still finds itself without a suitable product to plug this gap.

Meanwhile, an ambitious plan to manufacture and market tractors on foreign shores took shape. In the 1996-97 annual report, Rajan Nanda had referred to a pick-up in global demand for tractors, which could result in Escorts exporting 15,000 tractors a year over the next three to four years. To tap into this opportunity, a wholly owned subsidiary, Escorts Agri Machinery, was incorporated in the United States. This entered into two joint ventures, one with an American company, Long Agri Machinery, in 1998, and another with a Polish company, Pol Mot, in 2000, to cater to the American and European markets respectively. In the case of the United States, 70 per cent of the supply to Long Agribusiness (as the joint venture was named) was to be from Escorts and the rest from Korean company LG Tractors (part of the LG group, which got spun off as part of the LS group in 2003) and Italian company Same Duetz-Fahr. The joint venture in Poland involved assembling of semi knocked-down kits. Distribution arrangements in Turkey were finalised.

Action was not limited to the tractors business, however. Rajan Nanda wanted all businesses of Escorts to be firing on all cylinders. Escorts Yamaha Motor, managed by Anil Nanda, pushed out a slew of new products ranging from mopeds to motorcycles that were being snapped up in the market. Escorts Construction Equipment had acquired land in Ballabhgarh in Haryana in 1996 and started working on a new plant. And then came a major services push – first telecom, then healthcare and finally information technology (the last was not very significant, though).

Around 1994, Escorts was generating surpluses, and projections for the next three to five years indicated that the group would have the ability to invest more than Rs 200 crore. Rajan Nanda thought this would be a good opportunity for Escorts to diversify into new areas. Swaroop was tasked with identifying areas which the group could get into. One of them was fertilisers, since it was aligned with agriculture. Meetings were held with the Punjab government and a site identified. But a fertiliser plant was a capital-intensive project and, post liberalisation, there was uncertainty about the policy regime (fertilisers was a highly subsidised sector). The plan was dropped. Two other options remained on the table: power generation and telecom; both sectors had recently been opened up for private participation. Rajan Nanda chose telecom.

Escorts certainly seemed to be on a roll under Rajan Nanda. But there were problems lurking under the surface which made things go awry soon.

CHAPTER THREE

THE SWING INTO SERVICES

IT WAS PERHAPS natural for Rajan Nanda to choose telecom over power generation, though the latter was a more familiar sector for Indian industry. While both power generation and telecommunication were state monopolies prior to 1991, the former at least had a semblance of private participation in the form of captive power plants; in any case, it would have been more aligned with the Escorts association with manufacturing. Telecom, on the other hand, had no private participation before liberalisation, except in the manufacturing of telecom equipment, which Escorts was also into, through Escorts Communication Ltd.

But there was something tantalising about telecom – it was about new technology (something that always enthused Rajan Nanda) and it would also mark Escorts's venture into the services sector. There was a buzz about the telecom sector in the early '90s: the National Telecom Policy, 1994, which opened the door for the private sector in the communications sector, spoke about telephones on demand (something unheard of in India, where a telephone connection involved years of waiting, strings to be pulled or bribes to be paid) and an explosion in tele-density (which was not even 1 per hundred persons). In 1994, the government had floated tenders inviting bids for both basic telephony as well as cellular services.

Escorts did not participate in that round of bidding but started talking to global players eyeing the Indian market and scouting for local partners. In early 1995, it got into serious discussion with two companies – Northern Telecom of Canada (NTC) and GTE International Telecommunications of the United States. The board of directors gave the green signal for Escorts venturing into both basic telephony and cellular services. The talks with GTE progressed to the point where a company, Inditel Communications Private Limited, was incorporated. But GTE decided to stay away perhaps because it was still a bit sceptical of the Indian opportunity. That was also the last that was heard about basic telephony within Escorts.

A six-member core team led by Amulya Charan, who had joined some months earlier to head the telecom equipment manufacturing business, was set up to brainstorm on strategies for the telecom foray. Off and on, the team would get the sense that the chairman would not take the venture forward, Rajan Swaroop, who headed Escorts's strategic planning group and was a member of this core team, recalls. When Hong Kong-based First Pacific Company showed interest, Rajan Nanda was not very keen. At that time First Pacific was the second largest cellular operator in Hong Kong, with a presence in the Philippines as well. It had enormous confidence in the Indian market for cellular telephony. Thomas Y. Yasuda, managing director of First Pacific, came to India and had a meeting with Rajan Nanda; that meeting proved decisive in raising the latter's confidence levels about venturing into telecom. Escotel, a 51:49 joint venture between Escorts and First Pacific, was incorporated on 6 April 1995, with Escorts putting in Rs 200 crore as capital.

By then the government had started the second round of bidding and Escotel managed to get into the fray by the skin of its teeth; G.B. Mathur, company secretary, filed Escotel's bids for four circles on the last day of bidding. It won three, being the highest bidder for the West Uttar Pradesh (West-UP) circle and second highest for the Haryana and Kerala circles. The total licence fee it paid was Rs 485 crore. In addition, Escotel had to provide financial and performance guarantees to the Department of Telecommunications (DoT) to the tune of Rs 160 crore and had to raise debt for another Rs 204 crore. For all of these, Escorts Ltd provided corporate guarantees.

Around this time, Rajan Nanda decided that Escotel needed a new head. That was also the time Manoj Kohli, a vice-president at DCM Shriram, was looking for a change. Rajan Nanda called Kohli over to meet him, grilled him for two hours and gave him three options with just five minutes to decide: heading the tractors business, the JCB joint venture or the telecom business. Kohli, who was in his mid-thirties, chose telecom; his stint as CEO in Escotel was to make him a name to reckon with in India's telecom space.

Escotel had just about six employees when Kohli joined. They initially operated out of the office of Escorts Communication in Ballabhgarh, a town which is part of the Faridabad district and is also home to Escorts Construction Equipment. But the business needed to be more centrally located and Escotel moved into more swanky premises in Delhi's Mohan Industrial Estate area, not very far from the Escorts corporate headquarters. Rajan Nanda often visited the office and loved the open layout, the high levels of automation, the more relaxed and free vibe that was quite different from the stuffiness that still marked the manufacturing operations of Escorts.

What Kohli got was enormous freedom, perhaps more than those heading other businesses. Rajan Nanda was closely involved in the business but did not get into operational issues, perhaps because this was not an area that he was familiar with. Kohli, for his part, would consult him regularly on three issues: financial matters; regulatory issues and strategic or shareholder-related issues, mostly relating to First Pacific.

The immediate challenge was to achieve financial closure and Escotel was among the first of the licensees to do so. Services were launched in 1996 in all three circles. Kohli and his team focussed on the basics of the business – network quality, customer service and marketing. First Pacific deputed a British telecom industry veteran, Chris Edwards, as chief operating officer (COO), who proved invaluable in identifying the technology needed as well as the suppliers. Escotel was one of the few Indian companies to invest in its own microwave backbone transmission links in its circles[1] and its information technology systems were highly rated. The company quickly became known for the quality of its service and became the network of choice in the circles it was in. It was the first cellular company to adopt Six Sigma in key areas like billing, customer queries and complaints.

All this was supplemented by aggressive marketing. In Kerala, the challenge was particularly tough. Escorts never had a presence in the south, so brand recall was not high, and there was a language barrier too. What's more, it was up against BPL Cellular, whose promoters belonged to the state, though BPL was headquartered in Bengaluru. Kohli told the CEO of the Kerala operations to conduct all the marketing initiatives – billboards, signboards, messages, jingles – in Malayalam. 'Let them not think we are not Malayalis,' he said. The strategy worked; in one year Escotel's market share had gone up to 60 per cent. Some years down the line, Escotel also became the first company to launch an affordable rural mobile service. By 2001, it was the market leader in all the three circles it was in, not just in terms of customers but also revenues, and had become one of the jewels in the Escorts crown.

Financially, too, Escotel started doing well and, in 1998, it managed to negotiate new loan packages on the strength of its own balance sheet, without Escorts having to stand guarantee. It also attracted the interest of the investment community, with some insurance companies also keen to pick up a stake. Unfortunately, at a point when it was poised to soar, it passed up an opportunity which would have given it wings.

A company called J.T. Mobile, which had won the Andhra Pradesh and Karnataka circles, was looking to exit and wanted to sell out. The investment banking firm that held a substantial stake in it approached Escotel. Hyderabad in Andhra Pradesh and Bengaluru in Karnataka were the booming hubs of the new economy at that time and getting these two circles would have boosted Escotel's footprint. When an excited Kohli and Swaroop approached him, Rajan Nanda demurred; he felt it did not make sense. But with Yasuda also keen on going ahead, he gave the green signal for negotiations. Escotel met J.T. Mobile to get a sense of the asking price. When this figure was taken to Rajan Nanda, he turned down the possibility of acquisition. He was unwilling to bring the Escorts stake to below 51 per cent. Escotel had no choice but to withdraw. In late 1999, Bharti Cellular snapped up J.T. Mobile, giving its brand Airtel a huge leg-up. This refusal to dilute stake below 51 per cent (a deep-rooted fear of losing control, stemming from the corporate raid by Swraj Paul) was to come up twice later in the context of telecom and was to prove costly for the group as a whole.

Meanwhile, the telecom sector itself was in the midst of turmoil, with the companies that had got licences for cellular services facing financial strain and quite a few defaulting on their licence fee payments. Apart from bidding huge amounts as licence fee, the companies had also invested heavily in infrastructure. The operating costs were also high. However, the revenues generated were not as handsome as they had been projected to be (which is why the bids were so high). Call rates were prohibitive (people had to pay even for incoming calls) and this not only dampened sign-up by subscribers but also kept usage low; the revenue per user was much lower than expected. The private players also complained that delays in getting various clearances from the government disrupted their business plans. The sector petitioned the government, asking for a bailout and a more business-friendly policy.

In April 1999, the government unveiled a New Telecom Policy (NTP-99). Under this, the cellular operators moved from a fixed licence fee regime to a revenue sharing one; operators wanting to shift to the new regime had to pay whatever arrears they owed under the old regime. The licence period was extended from ten to twenty years. The Telecom Regulatory Authority of India (TRAI) was given the responsibility of tariff regulation and slashed call charges from Rs 16 a minute to just about Rs 6 a minute; increased competition brought the rates down further. This led to a surge in new subscribers as well as usage of mobile connections.

Capacities had to be ramped up to cater to this explosion in demand and the consequent exponential rise in traffic. First Pacific was excited by the opportunities that NTP-99 opened for the sector and wanted to expand. Yasuda was ready to bring in more investors or more partners into the joint venture. But Rajan Nanda's reluctance to give up controlling stake once again stood in the way.

Strangely, notwithstanding his reluctance to put in the kind of money that a capital-intensive operation like telecom required, Rajan Nanda was quite taken up with the idea of expanding Escorts's telecom footprint. By 1999, Escorts had divested or reduced its stakes in Escorts Yamaha Motors, Escorts JCB and Hughes Escorts Communications. That gave the company more management bandwidth and financial resources – around Rs 250 crore – to invest in core businesses, which were now identified as agribusiness, telecom, information technology and healthcare. The bulk of this Rs 250 crore was earmarked for telecom and information technology.[2] In the case of telecom, the plan was to acquire additional territories as well as launch data and internet services.

It was around this time that the unravelling of the Escorts telecom story – which would end up severely wounding the main tractor business – started.

In his Chairman's Message in the annual report of 2001-02, Rajan Nanda proudly declared that Escotel was all set to 'become our strongest retail chain with the largest numbers of channel partners, customer base and third most popular brand recall'. The company had an operating profit of 40 per cent of revenues.

But when the time for bidding for more circles came, Escorts decided to go it alone. A wholly owned subsidiary, Escorts Telecommunications Ltd (ETL), was incorporated in 2001. Though First Pacific believed in the enormous potential of the Indian market, it was facing financial stress back home. Bringing in a third partner would have helped. Nikhil Nanda also believed Escorts should limit its own exposure and bring in other investors. He, however, was unable to convince his father that 40 per cent of, say, a Rs 10,000 crore business was much better than 51 per cent of a Rs 1,000 crore one.

ETL bagged four circles – Punjab, Himachal Pradesh, Rajasthan and East Uttar Pradesh (UP-East). It had signed the licence agreement in October 2001 and had already done much of the preparatory work to roll out services in 2002-03. The licences, spectrum (the two were not bundled as had been the case when Escotel had got the first set of licences) and investment in infrastructure required an enormous amount of money. ETL had to resort to high levels of debt, which was guaranteed by Escorts. The bank guarantees on the balance sheet of Escorts for the telecom business soon amounted to nearly Rs 1,200 crore. The tractors business, which was ailing at that time, needed a lot of infusion of funds, but there was none to spare. Rajan Nanda was advised against this move by many people within and outside Escorts. But he was firm on going down this route and made light of these concerns: 'I've got the licences, this will bring in partners, everything is taken care of.'

That did not happen and eventually ETL never started operations in the four circles. First Pacific decided to exit Escotel for good, which meant Escorts had to find money to buy its stake. The 9/11 terrorist attack in New York threw global business in turmoil and the global telecom sector was particularly stressed. Escorts was negotiating with global investment banks, but was not getting the kind of valuation it thought it deserved. Then a deal was struck with the International Finance Corporation for $60 million in eight-year debt and $20 million for 49 per cent equity[3] but ultimately this, too, did not go through.

Kohli quit Escotel in 2002 and joined Airtel. Things started to go downhill quite fast, with Escotel starting to post operational losses. Meanwhile, Escorts was facing a severe financial crunch, with banks refusing to lend money for working capital for the tractors business. 'Sell telecom, get rid of the guarantees on your balance sheet and we will lend for tractors,' was a constant refrain Nikhil Nanda had to hear. There was no getting away from the fact that the telecom business – Escorts's first big foray into the services sector – would have to be sold.

After Kohli left, Swaroop was put in charge of the telecom business. He had initiated the move into telecom in 1994; nine years later he was given the responsibility of closing it.

There were regulatory issues to be dealt with. The government had recently allowed licences to be sold. In one of the first moves to get out of telecom, ETL sold its Punjab licence to Hutchison Essar, the Indian arm of the Hong Kong-based investment company Hutchison Whampoa.[4] Simultaneously, the search for a buyer for the whole business continued. Three years earlier, Birla-AT&T and Tata Cellular had come together to form BATATA (which later became Idea Cellular) and this combine emerged as a serious buyer. Though an MoU was signed, BATATA took its own time in closing the deal.

Meanwhile, the financial crisis in the Escorts group deepened. Tractor production had plunged from 5,000 a month to 500 and salaries were getting delayed. There didn't seem to be a solution in sight. One dull Friday afternoon, Nikhil Nanda was sitting in his office feeling very despondent. There were no lights – electricity supply had been cut off for non payment of bills.

'Is my dream of building upon this legacy going to die even as I am just starting my career?' he thought to himself.

Just then Umesh Banerji, the CFO, walked into his room. Banerji perhaps sensed Nikhil Nanda's mood and said gently: 'Nikhil, I am very sorry to bring you this news but we have tried everything and the telecom sale deal has been postponed to a point where the consortium bankers have told me they cannot give any more funds to keep the tractor numbers afloat. And if that can't be done, then the revenues to keep the business going are not going to come.'

Nikhil remembers this as one of the darkest moments of his life. When he went home that evening, his wife, Shweta, reminded him about an invitation to dinner at a friend's house. He told her: 'My world is falling apart. The last thing I want to do is to dress up and go out and smile.'

Shweta sat him down and told him that she empathised with what he was going through but in a crisis situation he needed to be brave and toughen up. He then decided to go to the dinner. It turned out to be fortuitous – by the end of the dinner, Nikhil had a very exciting offer from a telecom giant. So thrilled was he that he called Banerji from there at 12.30 a.m. to give him the news. The next morning, Nikhil and Banerji were at that telecom company's office for negotiations and the price agreed upon would have given Escorts far more than the Idea Cellular offer. Rajan Nanda and wife Ritu had been on a ten-day-long pilgrimage near Mangalore, where they could not be reached. When they returned, Nikhil presented him with a draft MoU setting out the broad contours of the sale. Rajan Nanda was very pleased and gave his son a rare compliment.

However, this deal could not be taken to its logical conclusion because of regulatory issues relating to the number of circles a player could be in. Later, Idea Cellular upped its offer. In 2004, Escotel and ETL went out of the Escorts fold. Escorts got Rs 205 crore and bonds worth Rs 175 crore payable by 2014.[5] This was the first exit from the services space. The healthcare business was now to follow.

STRICTLY SPEAKING, ESCORTS ventured into the services space in the '80s, in the area of healthcare. But at that time, healthcare was not seen as a business vertical. It was more of a giving-back-to-society activity that started with a chain of Ayurvedic hospitals in the '70s. The idea of such a chain occurred to HPN after he saw that villagers often preferred herbal medicines over allopathic ones but these were dispensed in unhygienic conditions. The well-equipped hospitals were attached to Escorts factories in Faridabad, Bengaluru and Patiala. They were, however, not limited to Escorts employees, but were open to the general public as well.[6]

In 1980, Rajan Nanda set up a twenty-five-bed general hospital, the Escorts Medical Centre, in Faridabad after some employees died because they did not get timely medical attention. A first for Faridabad, the Escorts Medical Centre too was open to the general public at affordable rates; Escorts employees paid only a nominal charge. But even as a philanthropic venture, Rajan Nanda was determined it would be the best. He lavished attention on it, ensuring it got the best facilities, doctors and other staff.

However, the venture with which Escorts made its name in the healthcare space was the Escorts Heart Institute and Research Centre (EHIRC) that was established in the mid-'80s. The idea was put to HPN by V.V. Purie, the proprietor of Thomson Press and film distributor. HPN realised that the country needed something on these lines; good quality cardiac surgery was out of reach of most Indians. For HPN, setting up a specialised heart institute served two objectives – helping Indians get access to quality care as well as providing good job opportunities for Indian doctors in the West who longed to return home.[7]

The EHIRC was registered as a charitable trust and it was funded through tax-free donations, 80 per cent of which came from Escorts. A three-member team was formed consisting of renowned cardiac surgeon Dr Naresh Trehan, the son-in-law of V.V. Purie; Dr Pervez Ahmed, son of former President Fakhruddin Ali Ahmed (both had given up successful careers in the United States to move back to India); and HPN's old associate Madan Agarwal, who had recently retired as head of the farm equipment division. Its brief: build the best cardiac hospital in Asia.

In November 1988, the hospital that would revolutionise cardiac care in India was inaugurated by then Prime Minister Rajiv Gandhi. Cardiac surgery in the private sector was not very robust in India. The few hospitals that did were prohibitively expensive. EHIRC standardised processes and put in place systems relating to practically every activity – from supply lines to streamlining movement of doctors and nurses in the operation theatre. Not only did this enormously add to the credibility of private healthcare in India that the Apollo chain of hospitals had brought, but it also reduced costs significantly. Suddenly, the middle class in Delhi had an option other than government hospitals. No expense was spared to get EHIRC the best equipment and technology. Soon people from outside Delhi started preferring EHIRC for cardiac surgery.

The opening of EHIRC did not mean that the Escorts Medical Centre was neglected in any way. Rajan Nanda continued to nurture it and, by the mid-'90s, it had become a 150-bed hospital. Dr N.K. Pandey, who joined the centre in 1985 and later rose to become executive director, recalls Rajan Nanda asking for review meetings with the doctors. There he would quiz them about the latest developments in various specialities that the hospital was offering and encourage them to bring in the latest technology – after satisfying himself that it was cost-effective and calculating the return on investment. If ever Dr Pandey cited lack of funds, that would be quickly brushed aside and Rajan Nanda made sure the hospital, which was a division of Escorts, was never short of funds.

By the mid-'90s, both the hospitals became self-sufficient. Around that time, corporatised hospitals were also growing in number in India, with the Apollo and Wockhardt chains being the better known ones. That is when Rajan Nanda started looking at the business potential of healthcare; in the annual report of 1999-2000, he listed it as one of the core businesses of Escorts.

In preparation for this, the Faridabad hospital was first converted from a division of Escorts into a wholly owned subsidiary, Escorts Hospital and Research Centre (EHRC), in 1998. With more focussed attention on it, as well as more resources, the hospital logged a 30 per cent increase in revenue in the first year itself. With a 78 per cent occupancy for its beds, expansion plans were put in place and, by 2002, it had become a 250-bed hospital.

The Heart Institute was then converted into a subsidiary of Escorts Ltd, renamed as Escorts Heart Institute and Research Centre Ltd (EHIRCL), with Escorts owning an 80 per cent stake, and the rest was held equally between Dr Trehan and Rajan Nanda in their personal capacity.

That done, it was time to take the brand further. Initially, EHRC and EHIRCL continued as independent entities but, in 2003, the former became a subsidiary of the latter. The five years from 2000 were the glory days of the healthcare business.

Soon after EHRC was converted into a wholly owned subsidiary, plans were put in place to expand it from a general to a super-speciality hospital, with cardiac care, kidney transplants and high-end orthopaedic surgery. EHIRCL's Delhi hospital got more beds and cath laboratories and the company got into managed contracts for cardiac facilities at several hospitals across the country, apart from setting up Heart Command Centres in and around Delhi. With many patients from other cities coming to the Delhi centre, new hospitals were opened in other states. EHIRCL established a strong presence in Amritsar and Raipur, started a Cardiac Care Centre in Kanpur and opened satellite centres in hospitals across the country. It also started working on a super-speciality hospital in Jaipur, along the lines of the Amritsar one. EHIRCL also notched up many firsts, including the country's first robotic surgery.

In order to fund expansion plans for the healthcare business, there was a plan to sell 25 per cent of EHIRCL's stake to fund the expansion of the hospital business. Of this, 17.1 per cent was to be from the Escorts holding of 80 per cent and the rest from the personal holdings of Rajan Nanda and Trehan.[8] Merlion India Fund, jointly owned by Standard Chartered and Singapore-based Temasek

Holdings, emerged as a serious buyer. Rajan Nanda believed EHIRCL would benefit from the association with Temasek.

However, this got torpedoed by an in-house missile. Even as Merlion India Fund was conducting its due diligence, Anil Nanda raised objections to the idea and challenged the corporatisation of EHIRC in court. Merlion India backed out.

Meanwhile, the financial position of Escorts kept worsening. The group had started defaulting on payments to banks, suppliers and dealers. Banks were not only reluctant to lend further to Escorts, some were even threatening to sell Escorts shares pledged with them as collateral against loans. The telecom business had been sold and, before that, Escorts minority stake in the joint ventures with Claas, JCB, Mahle and Goetze. In the case of JCB, Anthony Bamford had been keen that Escorts retain its 40 per cent stake. He acknowledged that JCB had become a force in India because of the connection with Escorts. Rajan Nanda was also not very happy about selling the stake in JCB – he had, after all, negotiated the joint venture. But Escorts needed the money and so the relationship came to an end with much sadness on both sides. There were some group companies and minority stakes in a few remaining joint ventures, but these would not fetch the kind of money needed to save the company; healthcare could.

That shook Rajan Nanda. This was a business close to his heart and had earned huge brand equity for Escorts among ordinary Indians. But he didn't have much of a choice: it was either this or letting the main tractor business go down, taking the entire business with it. Very reluctantly, Rajan Nanda agreed to sell Escorts's entire 80 per cent stake in the hospital business. The dream run came to an end for no fault of this business.

The sale was not easy, though several players in the healthcare sector found the company tantalising. After all, this was a respected brand with an almost pan-Indian presence and occupying prime real estate in most of the cities where it had hospitals. But the shadow of Anil Nanda's legal challenge to the conversion of the trust into a company loomed large and that put off some very strong healthcare and hospital brands that were interested. Finally, the Fortis chain, which was part of the home-grown pharmaceutical major, Ranbaxy, got into serious negotiations, helmed on the Escorts side by Shailendra Tandon, who had joined as CFO in 2004.

The negotiations were done in utmost secrecy, with red herrings thrown around aplenty to camouflage what was actually happening. At one point talks almost broke down when Fortis wanted to continue using the Escorts brand name tagged to Fortis after the sale and Rajan Nanda refused to entertain the idea. Tandon persuaded him, pointing out that Fortis would not harm the Escorts brand in any way and would only work to enhance it since it was going in for an IPO and that they would continue to nurture it even after that because Escorts was an iconic brand in the healthcare business. Finally, the deal price of Rs 650 crore was agreed upon. Escorts got Rs 520 crore, of which Rs 65 crore went into an escrow account.[9]

Now came the knotty issue of actual transfer of shares. A large chunk of Escorts shares in EHIRCL were pledged with three financial institutions and had to be released in order to transfer them to Fortis. A rather elaborate logistics exercise was planned in Mumbai (where the financial institutions and the share transfer office were located), with Tandon ensuring that the money Escorts owed to these institutions was deposited in their accounts and they gave a letter releasing the shares pledged with them. An Escorts employee was kept on standby with a car and, as soon as Tandon gave him the release letters, he was to go by car to Churchgate station in Mumbai and take the local train to the distant suburb of Virar, where another car was waiting to take him to the share transfer office. It was only after the share transfers were effected that the formal announcement was made, though the news had already leaked out to the business press about half an hour earlier.

As news filtered out, Anil Nanda and Trehan moved court challenging the sale. The very next day, the court ordered that all proceeds of the sale lying in the bank account would be frozen. Fortunately, on the day of the sale Tandon had already persuaded the bank to make out individual demand drafts in favour of sundry creditors (a list of all creditors and the amounts owed to them had earlier been shared with it) as soon as the money had come into the Escorts bank account. These drafts were with him before close of banking hours that day. He had not expected the legal challenge and the court stay but had done this only to make quick payments to creditors and send out a message that Escorts was a credit-worthy company. Because of this serendipitous development, the only money that got stuck because of the stay was what was to go to Rajan Nanda for his personal stake. Thanks to the demand drafts, Escorts was able to clear the dues of all to whom it owed money. The group had been saved.

Escorts involvement with healthcare did not end with this; it merely went back to the social activity it had started off as during HPN's days. The Escorts Medicare Foundation provides mobile medical units offering free consultation and medical assistance in and around Faridabad. It also operates a hub-and-spoke model through which it offers X-ray and diagnostics services, among others.

BY THIS TIME the writing on the wall was clear for the group's information technology (IT) business as well. This too had been an ambitious plan. That was the time of the software boom and many old-economy businesses were venturing into the IT space. As head of strategy, Swaroop had been talking to Rajan Nanda about this. In his Chairman's Message in the 1999-2000 annual report, Rajan Nanda had written: 'If the Indian industry is to succeed in the current competitive globalized scenario, there must be a right blend between the old and new economies.' He identified four core businesses for the group: agri, telecom, IT and healthcare. That was around the time Nikhil Nanda was getting more involved with the main business of Escorts and this was an area he started showing more interest in, intrigued as he was by the impact technology could have on how businesses would operate in the future.

The IT initiatives were launched through two new subsidiaries that were set up in 2000: Escosoft Technologies, which concentrated on software (entertainment software development and animation, enterprise software and IT solutions in the global market) and Esconet Services to e-enable other businesses of Escorts. Esconet, of which Swaroop was the CEO, got an equity infusion of around Rs 20 crore from Escorts and was structured into four businesses, each with its own CEO: Cellnext Solutions (which provided value-added services), iServ India Solutions (internet service provider), Automatrix India (an e-marketplace for the automobile sector using i2 Technologies) and a healthcare portal.

Both Escosoft and Esconet started off well, with the former setting up subsidiaries in the United States, United Kingdom and Singapore. iServ launched an internet telephony service, ZyberTalk in Delhi, and internet services in the three circles where Escotel was providing cellphone servies – Haryana, UP-West and Kerala. Cellnext, in which Nikhil Nanda was closely involved, developed text and multi-media messaging products for companies.

Unfortunately, Escorts had got into the IT arena late. Even as the companies were finding their feet and trying to grow, the dotcom bust of 2001 saw interest dying out. Both Esconet and Escosoft had planned to get some good partnerships and expand but this was no longer possible. Swaroop started focussing on building the businesses to add value but the dotcom bust showed such businesses would need large investments from the parent company and did not have a future. They were also losing money, though not so much as to harm the group. Cellnext was sold as a going concern to a Delhi-based mobile messaging firm. Automatrix and the healthcare portal got folded into existing businesses while iServ was wound down, and around 100 employees had to be retrenched – that was Nikhil Nanda's first unpleasant task.

Thus ended Escorts's brief flirtation with the new economy. It didn't entail huge financial losses for Escorts, as telecom had done, but it had affected management bandwidth. With Escorts exiting from these ventures, management attention could now focus much more on the traditional businesses. They were at a point where they needed that.

CHAPTER FOUR

SLIPPING INTO COMA

SOME TIME IN 2004, Rajan Nanda went down to Plant 1 where Powertrac tractors were produced. The normal bustle and noise of a fully functioning factory was absent. Production of tractors had come down to 6,000 a year in a factory that could roll out 72,000 a year. The company had posted a loss of Rs 314 crore. As he walked around the plant greeting workers, one of them made bold to ask: '*Sahib, company bech nahin rahein, naa* (Sir, we hope you are not going to sell the company)?' A shadow passed over Rajan Nanda's face before he gave a reassuring smile and said: '*Nahin, main hoon abhi, aap apna kaam karte rahiye* (No, I am still around, you carry on working).'

Did he feel as confident as he sounded? Neither the knowledge that unfounded rumours were rife about Escorts being up for sale nor having to face such questions would have been easy for the chairman of one of India's iconic business groups. After all, he had, along with his father, taken it to enviable heights.

So what had gone wrong?

The seeds of the troubles that Escorts faced from the late '90s were beginning to sprout even as Rajan Nanda was, soon after becoming chairman in 1994, making big plans for it to become a diversified conglomerate. The main challenge was increased competition following the opening up of the economy in 1991. A company that had operated in a closed business environment for over forty years found itself lagging in its response to a more competitive business environment. The BPR exercise to modernise the plants as well as make the workforce more productive had started only in 1996, and was just about getting off the ground when the stakes went up, with the entry of multinational companies.

In 1998, not only did a former joint venture partner, New Holland, launch its own tractor, but John Deere, a formidable name globally, also started its India operations. A few smaller players also made their debut. Not only were the multinational companies more efficiently run, but even domestic biggie Mahindra had got a head start in toning up its operations and systems in the late '80s and early '90s.

Around this time, the tractor industry started to sputter. Low agricultural prices and near drought conditions in Rajasthan and Gujarat in the late-'90s saw demand dip, especially in the northern and western markets where Escorts had a strong presence. The drought spread to more states and, compounding this, large food grain stocks with the government agencies saw a decline in procurement of food grains by the state-owned Food Corporation of India. This meant lower tractor sales, and capacity utilisation across the industry averaged around 50 per cent in the early 2000s.

By this time, there were twelve players in the market. From 1994-95 Escorts steadily lost market share, barring a one-year spike in 1999-2000 when the share increased to 20.1 per cent from 17.7 per cent the previous year.

Escorts could have salvaged something out of this situation if it had a tractor for the south in its stable. In 2000-01, while the tractor industry's sales for the whole country had fallen 10 per cent, sales in the south had increased 42 per cent. With no product for this market, Escorts could not take advantage of this growth. Mahindra and TAFE had been producing tractors for the south for long; Escorts had started work on it only in 1995. By this time, a dark horse entered the tractor market – Hoshiarpur-based International Tractors Ltd, which manufactures the Sonalika brand, run by first-generation entrepreneurs. Escorts viewed Sonalika with snobbish disdain. That proved to be a mistake. Though a late entrant into the market, Sonalika became the fourth largest manufacturer by 2005 and was nipping at Escorts's heels in the market share battle.

Escorts's dealers were even more ill-prepared for competition. They were accustomed to working in a seller's market where farmers would keep making the rounds of their showrooms asking about the status of their bookings. They were not able to make the switch to the aggressive selling that a more competitive market required.

To be fair, Chopra, as head of the farm equipment division, ensured that Escorts was not sitting on its hands. From 1996 onwards, along with the BPR exercise, it had been launching new series of tractors, especially in the horsepower ranges for which there was higher demand. A re-branding exercise saw differentiation between the premium Farmtrac, value-for-money and highly fuel-efficient Powertrac, and the rugged and economy-range tractors. Film stars Amitabh Bachchan and Sunny Deol were roped in as brand ambassadors. Serious efforts were made to mentor dealers to improve their performance. But this ramping up of production eventually did not go quite according to script. The combined effect of a market recession and loss in market share was that the company was left with huge inventory of unsold stock of around Rs 130 crore, leading to cash flow problems.

Payments to suppliers were delayed by six to nine months at times – overdues to suppliers touched Rs 250 crore by end 2005; people in departments dealing with them would avoid their calls. If supplies of raw material and components did not stop entirely, it was only because of the reputation Escorts had built up over the years and also because smaller suppliers in and around Faridabad saw Escorts as a benefactor and continued supplying to it. By this time, Escorts had over-leveraged itself on the telecom front, with Rajan Nanda's decision to go for the second round of licences without getting a partner on board, ignoring all advice to the contrary from within and outside Escorts.

So neck-deep in debt was Escorts that lenders were just not willing to engage with it. What particularly incensed them was the repeated assurance that the group was working on capital raising plans which would bring in around Rs 800 crore, which never happened. Chopra approached a top banker friend for a line of credit, only to get a friendly but firm snub. He had to devise innovative ways of raising finance to keep the tractor business going. One of them was to tap the dealer network. A few of them in each region were made stockists, which meant they would act as wholesalers who purchased tractors in bulk from Escorts, thus giving it some cash. They would then sell these to dealers and would be compensated by Escorts for the period they did not get paid by dealers. Though this scheme helped Escorts financially, it also contributed to the accumulation of unsold tractors with the stockist-dealers. In fact, many dealers gave up their Escorts business around this time.

THINGS WERE NOT much better in the other businesses. Escorts Construction Equipment Ltd (ECEL) faced a triple whammy. The construction industry faced a slowdown because of delay in implementation of various infrastructure projects by the government. Then the market was flooded with second-hand equipment following the completion of the Reliance India petroleum refinery in Jamnagar in Gujarat. And finally, it had to face competition from an erstwhile family member – Escorts became a minority partner in the joint venture with JCB in 1999 and then exited the joint venture in 2003.

The telecom equipment manufacturing business, which produced rural automatic exchanges and PABX systems, was also in the doldrums. The business head of Escorts Communication Ltd (ECL) quit in 1995 and Swaroop was asked to take charge. When he did, he found the factories idle. ECL managed to bag a few big orders from the DoT, and a technology collaboration with LG Information & Communication (LGIC) of South Korea was also attempted. But all this did not help very much. By 2000, the company's net worth had got eroded, resulting in it being referred to the Board for Industrial and Financial Reconstruction (BIFR).[1] Fortunately, Escorts got out unscathed – LGIC bought the company and Escorts did not lose any money. But that was one more business gone.

Even as the group was grappling with all this, it was hit by labour unrest twice in three years. The first was a seventy-day strike in December 1998 which was called after year-long negotiations on the respective charter of demands of the management and the union. This was the first time that Escorts had seen something so serious and was a test for Rajan Nanda's leadership. He came under tremendous pressure when the strike continued for more than a month because the entire industrial belt of Faridabad was affected. The strike hit all plants across businesses, and a majority of the smaller industrial units in Faridabad were suppliers to these. He, therefore, wavered over the management's tough stand. But Chopra insisted that the management should not back down.

The firmness paid off. The management and the union came to a landmark agreement in June 1999, which became the subject of case studies on industrial relations. While this ushered in a transformation of the work culture within Escorts, production and sales across businesses were hit to varying degrees. Unfortunately, the culture change did not last long and, in 2001, there was another strike that lasted eighty-four days. This time, the management buckled under and, from here on, the industrial relations became fraught, though there never was another strike.

Slowly Escorts started winding down its involvement in some of the joint ventures and later exiting from them. By 2003, Escorts had sold off its stake in Hughes Escorts Communications, Escorts Claas, Escorts JCB and Escorts Mahle. In 2004, the CEO of EACL and seven other employees bought out Escorts's 78 per cent stake in the company, making it one of the rare cases of management buyout in Corporate India. By now, Escorts was a pale shadow of what it once was. Over the next two years, the telecom and healthcare business were also sold. A group that straddled multiple manufacturing sectors was now limited to just three areas and its main business was in a comatose state. The tractor market had revived by then but Escorts had no money to produce tractors. The assembly lines hardly moved.

A FEW YEARS after the sale of the Escorts Heart Institute and Research Centre, journalist Bhupesh Bhandari asked Rajan Nanda whether he felt bitter about having to sell the telecom and hospital businesses. 'Not at all. You can't fight destiny,' was the blasé answer.[2] But it's a moot point whether it was only providence that was responsible for Escorts going out of kilter and mortal conduct had nothing to do with it.

H.P. Nanda's father,
Bhawan Ishwar Nanda

H.P. Nanda

A cartoon in *The Tribune* announcing the birth of Escorts in 1944

A range of early Escorts products

H.P. Nanda with his wife, Raj, and Raj Kapoor with his wife, Krishna, after the investiture ceremony of 'Das Grosse Verdienstkreuz'

The next generation: H.P. Nanda with his sons Rajan (left) and Anil

The Escorts Corporate Centre in Faridabad on the outskirts of Delhi

(From left to right) Nikhil, H.P. and Rajan Nanda – the men who have led Escorts over three generations

Rajan and Nikhil Nanda

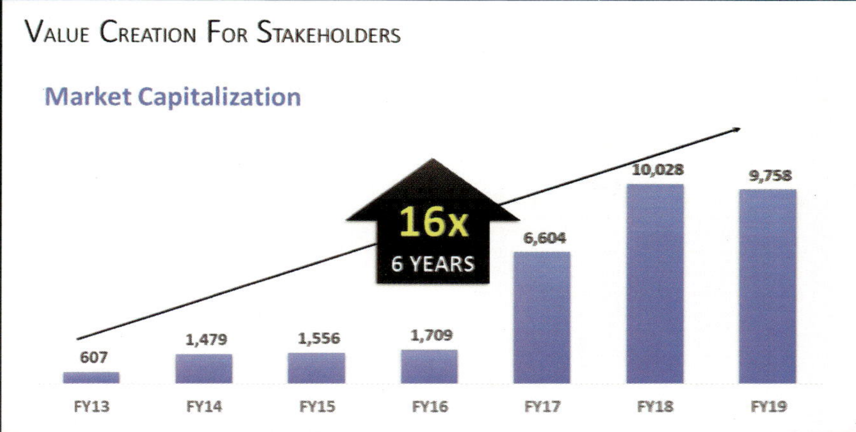

Escorts's market capitalization (in Rs crore) over the years

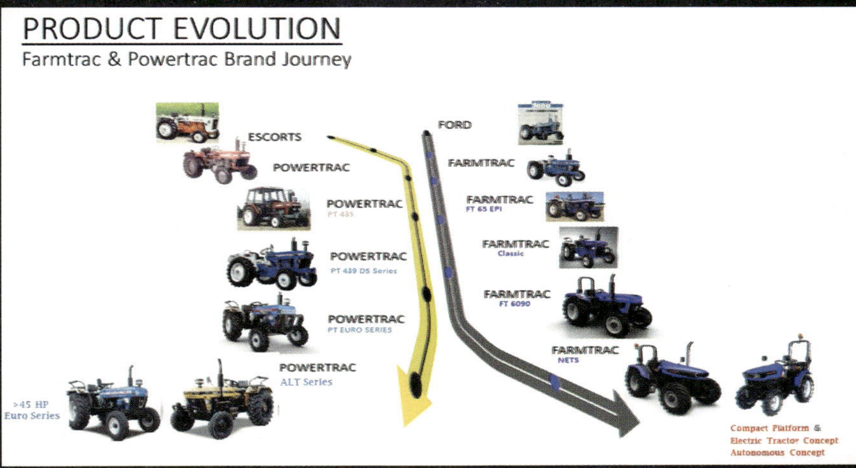

How Escorts tractors have evolved over the years

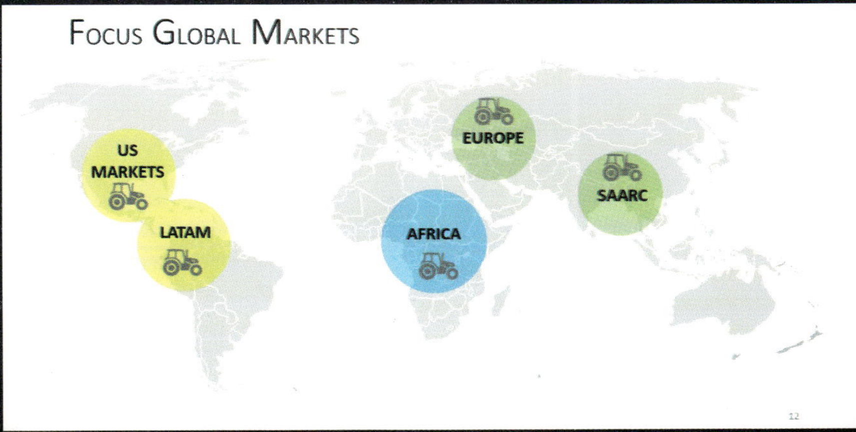

Escorts's global footprint

A range of recent Escorts products

Nikhil and Rajan Nanda meeting with Escorts suppliers

Nikhil Nanda meeting Escorts customers

Nikhil Nanda on
field visits

It is quite likely that the Escorts story may have panned out quite differently had Rajan Nanda's management style been a bit more consensual and collaborative than it was. His business acumen and his go-getting spirit were never in doubt, but even his staunchest defenders concede that his aloof persona, preference for dealing with only a small set of people and his distaste for interacting with the outside world affected Escorts during its troubled phase.

Unlike HPN, a gregarious, outgoing personality who would keep in touch with all stakeholders – from bankers and bureaucrats to suppliers and customers – Rajan Nanda just did not see the point of these interactions. 'In my father's time, he was establishing an industry, which meant he had to concentrate more on public relations. That is one thing I've stayed away from. I don't meet customers, I don't meet salesmen,' he very unapologetically told Bobb, in one of the rare interviews where he opened up.

He also did not encourage his top management to go out into the field. 'Why do you need to go? Don't you have senior executives to do this?' he was known to ask when he called for a CEO and was told he was out on a field visit. Annual dealer meetings were perfunctory and the ritual of annual supplier meets was abandoned. Dealers who had started their careers with Escorts in the late '60s were hurt that he did not remember their names and he barely paid attention when they spoke to him about the problems they were facing. Not only did this leave a crucial feedback loop open, but also left him clueless about developments in the market, something his father was always up to date about. A time came when he was not prepared to heed any negative reports and would dismiss them as rumours. He once even asked a new CEO of the farm equipment division who was planning to visit dealers to take the company helicopter, notwithstanding the incongruity of the CEO of a financially stressed company literally airdropping to visit dealers whose morale was already low.

He was reluctant to meet bankers too at a time when such meetings would have assuaged reservations of financial institutions. That was a pity because in the few meetings he did attend when Banerji forced him to, bankers were floored by his knowledge and grasp of issues. And, at a time when the Escorts share price started falling, meetings with the investor community were abandoned. In no time, Escorts went off the radar of investment banks and financial analysts.

Within Escorts, Rajan Nanda limited meaningful interactions to a small circle. His own son, Nikhil, who had become executive director in 2000, was not part of this select group. Even here, Rajan Nanda's style was not all-inclusive. Some like Banerji, Chopra and Manoj Kohli could speak their minds to him, though this was no guarantee that he would heed their advice. With others he could be a bit high-handed and this, inadvertently and inevitably, created a culture of sycophancy. Escorts lost a lot of good talent around that time. There was debilitating office politics and individual departments became independent silos that would not talk to each other. Reporting systems broke down. All this was to influence Escorts's path to recovery.

BY 2005, THE healthcare business had also been sold and Escorts had got out of the joint venture with Yamaha for motorcycles and Carraro for transmissions as well, apart from getting out of the information technology businesses. The proceeds of these brought debt down from Rs 886 crore in 2004-05 to Rs 649 crore in 2005-06. Escorts had been saved from bankruptcy but revival still appeared a distant dream. There was a lot that needed to be done and a lot of money needed to be pumped in.

Rajan Nanda started to feel Chopra was not doing enough. Chopra, for his part, was disheartened over the lack of money to revive the tractor business, which had begun to take a toll on him. A new CEO for the farm equipment division was brought in and Chopra was shifted to the corporate headquarters as head of corporate strategy. A month later he resigned; he had headed the division for over ten years.

Ashok Kumar Chadha, the new CEO, came with the strong recommendation of CFO Tandon, in whom both Rajan and Nikhil Nanda had immense trust. They had been colleagues at Indo Rama Synthetics. Chadha was the live wire that Escorts needed at that time. It was losing its self-belief at that point and he went around restoring it.

Soon after he joined, Escorts was looking at raising the next round of funds. Negotiations with a financial institution had been completed and the two parties had signed off on the dates by which the funds would be made available. But less than two months before that, the team handling this deal quit en masse to form their own company. The executive that the financial institution then appointed to the account said the process would have to start afresh. At a meeting with the company, Chadha was very firm – it should give a letter saying that it had failed to deliver on its signed commitment. Nikhil Nanda, who was present at the meeting, was taken aback at the firm stand Chadha took. But in doing that, Chadha sent out a message – stop taking Escorts lightly. The account moved to the new company which handled a Rs 150 crore QIP (qualified institutional placement) for Escorts.

Chadha, whose entry coincided with a pick-up in the tractor market, took this attitude everywhere. He was a workaholic who would come in to office around 8 a.m. and spend more than twelve hours there. He started insisting on daily meetings as well as production and sales planning. He would make audacious demands on suppliers, pointing out that he could clear their pending dues only if tractors were produced and sold. There were times he would land up at the factory at 4 a.m., going there directly from the airport. The shop floor started buzzing again. In two years, production of tractors had gone up from 1,000 a month to 5,000. The day that the 5,000 milestone was reached, Chadha gave everyone on the management team a bottle of champagne and a gift basket. New tractors for niche markets like orchards and vineyards were rolled out. He brought back market share to double digits – from 9 per cent in 2004-05 to 14.6 per cent the very next year. From Nikhil Nanda to senior executives to union leaders to dealers and vendors, the consensus is that without Chadha and his 'paradigm shift' motto, the Escorts story may have been quite different.

But paradigm shifts and shock treatments invariably have side effects. Unfortunately, the race to increase production led to a situation where the quality of tractors got affected, giving the Escorts brand a bad name in the market. Rajan and Nikhil Nanda found it difficult to reconcile with the idea of an Escorts which was almost forgotten but still spoken of with respect now being remembered with distrust. Three years after he joined, Chadha left the company. The search began for a new CEO for the tractor business. This was also a time when the competitive arithmetic started to go against Escorts. In 2005, TAFE had acquired Eicher Tractors and in 2007 Mahindra acquired the public sector Punjab Tractors Ltd, making Escorts's fight to get back to leadership position more difficult.

Almost immediately after Chadha left, a routine business decision revealed one action of his, in all probability taken in good faith, that landed the company in an expensive international arbitration.

In 2007, because of the weakening of the dollar by close to 14 per cent, Escorts had to cut back exports to the dollar markets, especially the United States. Though this was compensated by higher sales in Africa, Europe and South East Asia, the future of Farmtrac North America (as the erstwhile joint venture, Long Agribusiness, was named after Escorts became the majority owner) came into question. It did not make much business sense – the volumes were any way small beer. Talks were under way to sell Farmtrac North America to another company, but even as the potential buyer was doing its due diligence, Escorts made the mistake of publicly announcing its plans. The prospective buyer later backed off and that set off a calamitous chain of events.

Under the arrangement with LS Mtron (which had acquired LG Tractors in 2003), Farmtrac North America (FNA) would buy tractors from it on credit and sell to the dealers. The maximum credit at any point of time was $6 million. Chadha asked LS to increase the credit line to $12 million. LS said it would do so only if Escorts gave a comfort letter that it would pay up if FNA defaulted. Unknown to the chairman, Chadha issued the letter in March 2007, a few months before he left, the subject line of which termed it a 'guarantee letter', which gave it a legal sanctity. Perhaps he had never expected a situation where the letter would be invoked to arise.

Farmtrac North America also had a revolving credit facility with Textron Financial Corporation, the credit limit for which was $50 million. Chadha had got this raised to $80 million, saying that this could help Escorts appoint more dealers and push inventory and sales, again in an attempt to help the home company.

When news of the likely sale of Farmtrac North America broke, it set off panic among dealers and customers, and the sale of its tractors came to a near halt, shutting off its main source of funds. But it had liabilities worth several millions (including the LS and Textron credit lines) to repay. In November 2007, LS now invoked the guarantee that Chadha had given. When an already cash-strapped Escorts could not pay, the creditors took it to court and Farmtrac North America's assets were taken over by a receiver. Textron had the first lien on the assets and so got all the money from the sale (though that did not cover the entire money due to it). LS, knowing that Textron was the first claimant, had already moved the International Court of Arbitration, part of the International Chamber of Commerce (ICC), against Escorts and cited Chadha's letter to strengthen its claim. Before it did that, a representative of LS had met Rajan Nanda in Delhi while on a visit to India with a compromise offer. Nikhil Nanda and Rohtash Mal, CEO of the tractor division, had urged Rajan Nanda to accept the offer but he refused. After lengthy hearings, the ICC said Escorts should pay LS $7.172 million (the amount included interest and court fee). The order also said LS could lay a claim on any overseas facility that Escorts had and the company served a notice on the factory in Poland.

How the issue was resolved highlighted the generational change that was beginning to happen within Escorts. After the order of the ICC, lawyers representing Escorts told the management it did not need to act on it. Implementing orders of foreign courts in India was extremely difficult, they assured, and advised the company to file an injunction in an Indian court against LS. This was a standard move for many Indian companies and had sullied India's reputation in the global arbitration world.

However, Nikhil Nanda, who was by now joint managing director and was beginning to make his voice heard, put his foot down. His logic was simple: Farmtrac North America was a step-down subsidiary and, regardless of Chadha's letter, the company did owe LS. More importantly, not honouring the ICC court award would tarnish Escorts's reputation globally. Why, he asked Rajan Nanda, should Escorts be spending Rs 4 crore a year on legal fees for a battle that it was bound to lose and would imperil any global plans it may have? He strongly argued for a compromise with LS. Rajan Nanda, however, did not heed his advice.

Nikhil Nanda then escalated matters to the board. At a meeting in February 2015, after the agenda items had been completed, he said, 'With the chairman's permission I want to make a statement.' Rajan Nanda was taken aback but had to allow him. Nikhil quickly sketched out the background. He then said: 'There is a difference of opinion between my chairman and me and I want your advice and mandate. I think if we don't repair this relationship, not only will we destroy our image but also not be able to create any future outside India.' Two directors immediately said, 'You have our mandate, please go and negotiate.'

Nikhil Nanda quickly wrote to Kwang-woo Lee, president and CEO of LS-Mtron, requesting a meeting. He acknowledged that LS would find it difficult to trust Escorts but had only one request – that Lee should keep an open mind, since Escorts was coming with an intent to resolve. The meeting in Singapore in March 2015 was an exhaustive and exhausting one. Finally Nikhil proposed a phased repayment plan, where 50 per cent of the amount would be given right away and the rest in three instalments over three years. The last instalment was paid in September 2018.

'HISTORY WILL JUDGE Rajan Nanda more harshly than he should be,' believes Chopra. Judged on the basis of balance sheets and results, no doubt the Escorts empire shrank during his tenure. But if it were not for the fact that he over-leveraged himself financially, he points out, Rajan Nanda would have been hailed as a master strategist who diversified Escorts successfully into the services business. There is another reason Chopra is right. Corporate India's history is replete with instances of blue-chip family-run businesses being run aground by second- or third-generation leaders. But instances of their actively and seriously trying to revive them are few and far between. There was no incentive to do so because, till the Insolvency and Bankruptcy Code debuted in 2017, a company going bankrupt made not an iota of difference to the lifestyles of its promoters. Rajan Nanda could have done the same. The assurance he gave the worker at Plant 1, however, showed he was of a different mettle – he knew the company had come to this pass under his stewardship and he was determined to steer it back to good health. He started doing just that, working with his son and others he had disregarded. He could have walked away from it all. He did not.

CHAPTER FIVE

THE CLAW BACK

IN SEPTEMBER 2013, Nikhil Nanda sat in his office looking at his grandfather's ring, which his father had, a few hours earlier, placed on his finger while announcing his elevation as managing director. HPN had willed the ring to his younger son, Anil, who had later given it to Rajan Nanda saying that their father was blessing them through this. For Nikhil Nanda, the gold ring with a single diamond was more than just a blessing; it was something he would draw strength from as he steered Escorts back to the glory days of his grandfather's time; he felt HPN was speaking to him through that. As he prepared to grapple with Escorts's many problems, it also reminded him of his mother's words: gold has to go through the grind to shine.

The Escorts he had just become managing director of was but a pale shadow of what it once was. When he had joined the business in 1995, at the young age of twenty-one soon after his return from college in the United States, Escorts straddled multiple businesses, his father had just become chairman and was restructuring the group to take it to greater heights. But now the company was down to just four businesses, which also were not in the best of health. It was slowly getting out of a near-bankruptcy situation. Some years earlier, Shweta had told him she had heard about a banker friend's snide remark to another friend: 'How can Nikhil and Shweta come to our homes and socialise with us, when his company owes us money?' Nikhil, whom his mother and wife describe as extremely sensitive, felt gutted and, apart from drastically curtailing his socialising to just a few very close friends, he resolved, 'I am H.P. Nanda's and Raj Kapoor's grandson. I am here with a purpose, I may fail in my endeavours, but I am going to give a fighting response.'

That resolve had a context. Both grandfathers had fought their way back after debilitating setbacks. HPN had brought Escorts back from the brink of death twice – once after Partition and the second time after the Swraj Paul hostile takeover episode. Maternal grandfather Raj Kapoor, the iconic thespian, had faced financial ruin when his rather intense film *Mera Naam Joker* bombed at the box office in 1970. Three years later, his fortunes revived when he returned with the trend-setting teenage romance *Bobby,* which had the highest box office collections that year and was among the top grossers of the '70s.

Nikhil realised, at the same time, that reviving Escorts was not going to be easy and that the battle would be on multiple fronts, including with his own father.

IT WAS PERHAPS a given that Nikhil would join the family business after he finished college – the first in three generations to have graduated. He wanted to stay back for a year or two in New York and work in an investment bank. But HPN and Rajan Nanda had insisted that he return. So he first spent eight months training with JCB in Britain before returning to join the family business.

Like his grandfather and father, Nikhil harboured a deep and undying passion for Escorts. People who have seen all three generations say Nikhil has a great deal of his grandfather in him, but there are crucial differences as well. Both HPN and Rajan Nanda were forceful personalities, while Nikhil is mild to the point of being self-effacing. He is not gregarious and expansive like HPN, but reserved by nature, like his father. And yet, he makes a conscious effort to overcome this when it comes to interacting with external stakeholders, something Rajan Nanda loathed. The way father and son interacted with people within Escorts is also markedly different. Rajan Nanda preferred to interact with a small set of advisers. Nikhil is far more collaborative and consensual in his approach. In his early years, he spent a lot of time listening to people. That was how he started to make a difference to the way Escorts was being managed, though his innate diffidence perhaps lost the company valuable time.

Nikhil's first assignment in Escorts was at the Yamaha motorcycle division in 1995. He started in a corporate position and not in an operational role like his father had done. Once the Escorts Yamaha Motor Ltd joint venture was formed, he shifted to Escorts Ltd in 1997 as director. But he didn't have very much to do and he pretty much watched from the sidelines as his father fired on all cylinders. HPN involved Rajan Nanda early on in the business because he was building it up and needed a trusted person to handle the operations. By the time Nikhil was old enough to shoulder responsibilities, Rajan had a lot of professional expertise available to him and so it perhaps never occurred to him to involve his son the way his father had involved him, though close advisors did tell him to. Father and son doted on each other but, in the office, Rajan Nanda happily sidelined Nikhil and the latter always addressed him as Mr Chairman or Sir. Nikhil was given responsibility for the group's foray into the information technology space but that was a very small part of the overall Escorts empire and it lasted for less than two years.

Though Nikhil became executive director in 2000 and attended key meetings, his active participation was never encouraged. So he just observed, watching with concern as the company started its steady slide downwards. It took a crushing encounter with an investment bank for him to decide that he would not be a silent, helpless bystander any more. At this meeting at the Belvedere Club in The Oberoi in New Delhi, Nikhil noticed that the bankers were not even listening properly while the Escorts team was making its presentation. After around twenty minutes, one of the bankers present looked at Nikhil and said: 'Escorts is gone. We can cut you a cheque to walk out gracefully.' This was far worse than the friend's remark; that had been made behind his back, this was being said to his face and in a professional setting. Nikhil told him he was not there with a price tag for Escorts. 'With all due respect, you have had a chance to say what you just did, but you have just strengthened the resolve that I always had. Enjoy the coffee and we will meet again in the near future,' he said before walking out of the meeting.

That was the first watershed moment for his involvement in Escorts. He quietly started identifying people who, he felt, genuinely wanted the company to do well and talked to them to understand why things were going the way they were, attempting to become a conduit for their thoughts and ideas. In the telecom business, for example, he was vocal in wanting Escorts to bring in more partners into the venture instead of relying so heavily on debt. Slowly, people outside his father's circle started opening up to, and confiding in, him. He came to know about information being withheld from the chairman and rosy pictures being presented to him, lack of compliance with processes and much more.

The second watershed moment and one that saw him evolve as a manager was the negotiation with the telecom major that he had initiated. It was the first time his father was very happy with something he had done on the business front. It also gave him the confidence that he could play a far more significant role in the company. From around 2005, he started being a bit more assertive, though not as much as a lot of people expected him to be.

There were occasions when he did manage to make a difference. One of the smaller businesses had been bleeding heavily and Nikhil told the chairman that the CEO needed to go. The senior Nanda agreed, but did nothing about it. A few months later, Nikhil walked into his father's room and said, 'Mr Chairman, I think you need to set an example that we mean business. I suggest you call him and give him your decision about his exit.' Rajan Nanda looked at him for a few seconds and then said, 'I am not going to do it, you do it.' That floored Nikhil; he had not expected that level of acceptance by his father, though he was joint managing director.

Nevertheless, armed with the go-ahead, he called the CEO for lunch and grilled him on the much-promised restructuring plan. When all that he kept getting in return was vague excuses, he cut the CEO short and said: 'This is not the tone or leadership that we want in the company. You need to leave.' The shocked CEO asked him whether he had the authority to sack him. Nikhil responded that he had twenty-four hours to leave on his own and that the decision was backed by the chairman as well as the human resources department. More than the exit, it was Nikhil's role in it that sent shockwaves through Escorts.

BY 2005, RAJAN NANDA had also accepted the need for drastic action in order to get Escorts out of the rut it was in. Getting finances back on track was a top priority. Banerji, the CFO whom both father and son held in extremely high regard, had retired in 2004 and Tandon was brought in a few months later. Deference was not one of Tandon's qualities and he did not shy away from speaking his mind. What he noticed within days of joining was that there was a complete breakdown of financial discipline and lack of communication between the corporate divisions and the individual businesses. Tandon started shining the light on these, including issues having financial implications on the company.

Some pressure had eased with the sale of the hospital and information technology businesses and stake in Carraro India as well as the completion of the process of sale of Escorts Telecommunication to Idea in June 2006. But Escorts was still nowhere close to being out of the woods. A major task was to win back the trust of lenders – post-dated repayment cheques for even relatively small amounts had bounced. Executives in the finance department were told to park themselves in the offices of bank managers and not leave till they got sanction letters for new credit lines. Among them was Bharat Madan, who had recently joined after quitting a multinational company, Electrolux Kelvinator, and worried about what he had got himself into. The persistence paid off and three banks – Axis Bank, State Bank of India and Bank of India – each gave a credit line of Rs 50 crore each. It was thanks to these banks that Escorts managed to keep operations going. Without this lifesaver, no amount of dynamism on Chadha's part would have had any tangible effect.

Tandon, who had stitched together the healthcare sale deal, worked on getting some semblance of financial discipline and harmony in place, introducing new formats of reports submitted to the corporate office by individual departments within specified timelines. This gave the top management a clearer idea of what was going on in individual departments; business heads could no longer sweep problems under the carpet. The setting up of audit committees within the board of directors had become compulsory by then and Tandon used this opportunity to voluntarily share a lot of information with the directors, which increased the scrutiny of the management by the board. But before he could put in place more processes and systems – most of his tenure had gone by in fire-fighting – he left, after spending less than three years with the company and a few months before Chadha's exit. Over the next five years, there were a succession of CFOs but they all proved ineffective; in fact, one was found to be slandering the company. It was this that prompted Nikhil, who had been very unhappy over Tandon's exit, to decide that grooming in-house talent was the way forward.

When, in 2011, his father had interviewed yet another potential CFO who had demanded a huge pay packet, Nikhil asked why he did not think someone from within the company could do the job. As Rajan Nanda demurred, he argued that it was important to give people within the company the hope that they too could move up in the hierarchy. A day or two later, he invited Madan to his room for lunch and told him that he saw him as a potential CFO. 'Are you aligned and committed? Are you willing to do what it takes to give the chairman the support he needs?' Madan immediately said yes.

In end 2007, the tractor division got a new head, Rohtash Mal, who was given the title of executive director and CEO. Mal came from process-driven companies like Maruti Suzuki and Airtel. For Escorts, this was a good management progression – Chadha had pulled the company out of paralysis, Mal would take forward the process of institutionalising processes and systems that the company so sorely lacked and needed. Importantly, it also sent out a message to the world that Escorts had started attracting pedigreed executives and that it was getting its act together.

Mal had known that Escorts's recent history was troubled but had not expected the Augean stables that he encountered. Every day his 300-square-foot waiting room was filled with complaining suppliers, dealers and bankers; they had all come without an appointment. The managing director of a major tyre supplier walked into his room one day with a cheque that had bounced. Dealers were furious about the poor quality of tractors which resulted in their facing the ire of the customers. There was indiscipline on the shop floor and thefts were taking place in the factory. Employee morale was at rock bottom. And adding to all this, there was extremely vicious politics at the corporate office. Top executives did not seem to care about the company; when he asked one what the priority to revive the company should be, he was told that people were not happy with the executive lunch after the non-vegetarian menu was withdrawn!

He had to battle on multiple fronts; two key people in his team were Madan and Shenu Agarwal, who had been heading Farmtrac North America. Shenu had started his career with Escorts in 1994 and Nikhil had wooed him back to India after Farmtrac North America had closed. Madan and Shenu became vital members of what would, over time, become Nikhil's resurrection team. Mal leaned on Madan a great deal to tackle the many knotty financial issues. Shenu was designated head of strategy in Mal's office and was the pointsperson for fourteen projects that he initiated, on issues ranging from cash conservation to product development to marketing initiatives.

Mal realised early on that it was important for him to navigate carefully through the minefield of office politics. The best way to neutralise the negative elements, he and Nikhil agreed, was to show up their ineptness in an incontrovertible way and have them fall from grace. The various projects he initiated often offered chances to do so. One of them was the Strategic Cost Reduction Exercise (SCORE).

One target in SCORE was to save Rs 50 crore on plant operations. The head of operations was asked about the monthly consumption of diesel. He did not have a clue. It was later discovered that leakage of compressed air in the pipes in the plant was pushing up diesel bills. Fixing the leaks led to a saving of Rs 5 crore a year. That this had gone undetected was a big blotch on the reputation of those responsible for operations till then.

Other actions were far more dramatic and surgical in their impact; Nikhil was in the loop on all of them. Mal found that he was actively discouraged from visiting the shop floor. But he started going there regularly nevertheless and, as he walked around, he noticed cobwebs behind the circuit breakers and workers who were unshaved and not in uniform, just sitting around. He kept Rajan Nanda informed about these. One day, he saw that the mezzanine made of slotted steel, where tools would be stored, was covered with cobwebs. When he asked for it to be cleaned, he was met with much humming and hawing and told to leave it. He insisted and, when the mezzanine was cleaned, close to a hundred empty liquor bottles were found – workers had been drinking while on duty.

The very next day, Mal summoned a senior executive in the manufacturing department who was considered part of Rajan Nanda's charmed circle. He gave him two letters. One was an unsigned resignation letter and the other was a letter terminating his services. He was asked which one he would prefer. The executive took both the letters and went to see Rajan Nanda. Mal had not consulted the chairman on this but, given the evidence, the chairman declined to intervene. Shailendra Agrawal, who had started his career with Escorts and had moved to Hero Motors in 2005, was brought back to replace him. He too would later become part of the resurrection brigade.

A similar strong signalling action was needed to eliminate corruption in the purchase and accounts department. When vendors alleged that bribes were being sought to release payment cheques, strong action was taken, including dismissals. This sent out a clear message about zero tolerance. There was, at the same time, recognition that merely striking fear in the hearts of the corrupt would not suffice; processes that eliminated scope for such corruption were also put in place.

In yet another signalling move, an executive who was found fudging travel bills was also dismissed. It was a minor issue that happens in all offices, but the motive was to drive home the point that even minor transgressions would not be tolerated.

Work, meanwhile, continued on restoring the financial health of the company. Wooing back the confidence of lenders was not easy. Too much damage had been done because of loans being taken on the basis of unreal projections. Mal went to see the executive of a financial institution which was the head of a consortium of lenders. So devalued had Escorts become that he was kept waiting for a long time despite a scheduled appointment. He admitted that the past record of the company did not inspire confidence, but persuaded the executive to look beyond the balance sheet and at the way the top management planned to set things right. It was only after sitting through a three-hour-long presentation at the Escorts office, which underscored the sharp plans and deep-seated commitment of the team, that she spoke to the other bankers and kept the credit lines open for another six months. Alongside, a major financial re-engineering exercise was undertaken with the help of consulting firms. Over two years, the balance sheet was completely cleaned up, putting Escorts on firmer ground.

Mal also got the top management of Escorts to start engaging with the investor community, something it had not been doing. In 2009, a dedicated investor relations cell was set up, after the share price fell to Rs 30 in December 2008. The market capitalisation also came down to Rs 319 crore in 2009, though it bounced back the following year to touch four digits – Rs 1,573 crore – for the first time since 2000.

Meanwhile, there was a lot of action on the production and product development front. A Quality Push Mission focussed on improving manufacturing efficiencies, material costs were reduced, the first ever inverter tractor was launched along with several higher horsepower ones, new marketing initiatives were launched and the company bagged India's largest ever single export order in Africa worth $40 million. Planning also started on providing farmers with end-to-end solutions, from preparing the land to harvesting the produce.

All this would not have been possible, though, without one landmark initiative, which proved to be a watershed in the revival of Escorts.

While discussing organisational development with consulting firm PricewaterhouseCoopers, Mal, who knew it was crucial to restore the sense of self-belief in Escorts, heard about a technique called large scale interactive process (LSIP), which is meant to align disparate stakeholders – vendors, dealers, customers as well as employees – of large organisations to a common goal. He quickly latched on to the idea and got Shenu Agarwal to give it shape, apart from putting together a ten-member team. This was needed because there were watertight silos – research and development, operations and sales and marketing at the corporate level – that hampered alignment of objectives. Mal did manage to knit them together, but much more was necessary.

'*Khud ko karo buland* (let's make ourselves stronger)' was the theme of the three-day event called Sankalp in Plant 1 in 2009. A large makeshift hall was put up on the grounds of the plant and close to 2,000 employees, across ranks, participated. A few customers, suppliers, dealers and bankers were also invited. The first day was just about venting. Workers complained about lack of facilities, managers complained about broken chairs and air-conditioners being switched off at 4 p.m. to save power, suppliers complained about managers taking bribes to let trucks enter and a customer displayed a gunny sack full of broken parts from a four-year-old tractor. Rajan and Nikhil Nanda then shared how important the company is to them as well as to the larger community and the country, outlining their vision for the future of the company. The chairman's voice choked a couple of times as he recalled the glory days of the company. '*Maine bhi galtiyan ki hain* (I have also made mistakes),' he said. Mal's war cry was '*Izzat waapis*' (regain respectability). '*Lakshmi kahaan jaati hai? Jahaan izzat hoti hai. Vahin paisa aata hai, samriddhi hoti hai* (Where does the goddess of wealth go? Where there is respectability and prosperity).

Once the external stakeholders left, it was a free for all, with individual departments blaming each other for the state of affairs. Lathe operators complained that the managers did not give spares; the managers blamed the purchase department for delays. That done, it was time to acknowledge that everyone was at fault and solutions would have to be worked out jointly. Employees were grouped around tables, each with a coordinator, and given large sheets on which they listed the top two 'GLADS, SADS and MADS' and the top two consequences if Escorts did not change. These were then tacked on to the walls of the hall. Quite a few charts acknowledged that this would be the end of Escorts and their livelihoods if there was no change. People were then encouraged to come on stage and speak about what each of them would do to bring about this change. Sankalp, the name of the programme, means pledge, and several pledges were taken over those two days. Particularly significant was the fact that union leaders, who had a huge hold on the workers, vowed to do something. Escorts had turned the corner psychologically.

Silos did not disappear nor did discipline return to the factories overnight. What Sankalp did, however, was to make it easier for the management to tackle these problems. Among the early things Mal did, capitalising on the post-Sankalp enthusiasm, was to replace the company's own security guards with private security firms. This was not easy, since the guards were members of the union. One day he went to where some components were being unloaded. When the supplies were counted, thirteen pieces were missing. A few days later, he called the union president, S.D. Tyagi, and told him respectability would not be restored if this continued and that security would have to be outsourced. When Tyagi objected, he proposed that the security guards would be absorbed in other positions in the company. Gradually, with Nikhil's unstated and unstinting support, Mal and the industrial relations team worked to bring about a sea change in the attitude of workers and the union, using a carrot-and-stick approach. This was also the period when a lot of emphasis was laid on investing resources in people. Nikhil's decision to groom home-grown talent was not limited to top executive positions but across the company hierarchy. Twenty-odd individuals were identified as potential leaders and mentored.

By 2010, the Nikhil Nanda–Rohtash Mal team had finished rescuing the company. When Mal had joined, Escorts had posted a loss of Rs 6 crore in 2006-07; by 2010-11, it was well on the path to sustained profitability. The SCORE initiative had resulted in a savings of more than Rs 100 crore. However, the institutionalisation of Escorts, something Nikhil was keen on, remained an unfinished task. Mal had worked on a blueprint for the next decade, in close consultation with Nikhil. In July 2011, he presented the plan to Rajan, Nikhil and Nitasha Nanda (Rajan Nanda's daughter). But he was due to retire in March 2012, and though Nikhil would have preferred that he get an extension, that did not happen. Search began for a new head for the agri-machinery division.

BY THIS TIME, Nikhil had gained a bit more control, but it took some strong action at ECEL for the organisation to realise that he was not to be taken lightly any more.

ECEL accounted for less than 15 per cent of Escorts revenues but had never been a serious cause for worry; in fact, it had been one area where Escorts had maintained a strong performance. But that changed from 2010 onwards, with the industry itself facing a slowdown. The infrastructure sector came to a near standstill, thanks to, first, the global economic slowdown of 2008 and then the policy paralysis that had set in within India after 2011. ECEL started slipping into losses. Nikhil kept flagging this to the chairman, pointing out that the CEO of ECEL was not very effective. But it took more than a year for Rajan Nanda to concede that Nikhil was right and give him full freedom to restructure the construction business.

In 2011, ECEL was merged with Escorts, mainly to derisk the parent company from the vagaries of rainfall-dependent agriculture – a lean agricultural season invariably meant lower tractor sales – and also to slowly transition it into an engineering company by tapping into the infrastructure story. But the merger also brought Escorts under scrutiny from the investor community. Along with ECEL, Escorts Finance Investments and Leasing (EFILL) and Escotrac Finance and Investments were also merged with Escorts. The shares of all these companies were converted into treasury stocks and housed in a separate trust, the Escorts Benefit and Welfare Trust. But the beneficiary of the trust was the company, which could use the proceeds from the dividend and sale of shares for its future growth. Nevertheless, this angered the minority investors who expected the shares to be cancelled. However, the merger was approved by the courts and later got the approval of the shareholders too.

Following the merger of ECEL with Escorts, Nikhil started chairing the management committee meetings of the construction division. He soon realised that he was being presented the same airbrushed rosy pictures that his father used to be given. He started questioning the figures being given and the assumptions being made. Realising this was getting him positive vibes from others present in the room who had been silenced earlier, he encouraged them to speak up. When the embroidered presentations continued after a few meetings and he also realised that games were being played with him, he decided enough was enough. He had given them a long enough rope and now decisive action could not be delayed. One day, he left the meeting abruptly, walked to his father's room and said he would not be able to restructure the business without changing people. Rajan Nanda told him to do what he wanted to. Before returning to the meeting, Nikhil briefed the human resource department. He then walked into the room and told five people that they had twenty-four hours to leave or they would be sacked on grounds of harming the company through misinformation.

Similar actions followed in the railway equipment division. All this could have backfired by creating insecurity, but the fact that he had been encouraging the more positive people worked in his favour. More of such people started coming forward and speaking up which, in turn, gave him confidence that there was enough talent within the company to turn it around.

The merger of ECEL with the parent company was described as part of the move to create 'one company, one culture'. There was a growing realisation that it was not enough to just break silos within individual businesses and that the group's strengths needed to be leveraged for all of them. Besides, each business had its own CFO, human resource heads and information technology systems, leading to a lot of duplication as well as underutilisation of human and financial resources. The finance function, for example, had 260 employees across four businesses.

A start had been made in 2010, with the consolidation of enterprise resource planning (ERP) in various divisions into a common ERP platform. Called Sangamam (which means confluence), this involved integration of, among others, individual purchase, material, manufacturing, sales and warehouse management modules into the common ERP platform. The idea was to control costs as well as enable the top management to keep track of parameters like inventory, production and cash flow, increasing transparency.

This did not meet too much resistance. Doing the same for the finance and human resource functions was not easy. One, nobody wanted to give up their individual turfs. Two, disparate finance departments offered a lot of scope to misrepresent the performance of an individual business, because of which the corporate office never had a clear picture of how much money was needed every month to run the businesses. Meetings related to finance would often descend into different divisions contesting each other's figures. Tandon and Mal had improved the reporting of finances so that the corporate office got a better grasp of how much cash was available with the company; a common finance department would take this process forward.

Ultimately the management bit the bullet and created a shared services centre in which, to start with, the finance function was integrated under Madan as CFO. With this, the number of employees in the finance department came down to 160. Over a period of time, this function was outsourced and the number of employees in the centralised finance department came down to just seventy. But, more importantly, the numbers started presenting a more realistic picture than earlier. This was followed by centralisation of the materials department as well as of research and development. What this led to was better working capital management and more disciplined treasury management. Slowly, the group's EBIDTA margin started improving – from 4.7 per cent in 2011-12 to 6.4 per cent in 2013-14.

The recovery was well under way. It now needed to be nurtured and built upon.

CHAPTER SIX

POWERING AHEAD

THE BATON THAT Rohtash Mal left when he retired as executive director and CEO of the agri-machinery division was picked up by Sambandhan Sridhar, who had been working in Bajaj Auto as president of the motorcycles division. By this time, Rajan Nanda had started to acknowledge that his son was making a difference to the way the company was being managed and both were in greater alignment than before. They started to agree on a number of hires at the senior management level; Sridhar was one of them. A year later, they picked Dipankar Ghosh, who was vice-president of the John Deere Technology Centre in India, to head the railway equipment division. Between them, these two CEOs brought in a lot of great talent from outside – the turning of the talent tide that had started with Mal's entry in 2007 had become decisive now.

After the initial interview that both Rajan and Nikhil Nanda conducted, the latter went over to Pune, where Sridhar was based, and had a long session with him, asking him about his values and what drove him. Nikhil had gelled very well with Mal and they had worked in close partnership. With Sridhar, he felt a greater connect and this would be key to speeding up the process of revival.

When Sridhar joined, Escorts was going through an identity crisis of sorts. He put an end to that. Before joining he had done some research and found that people still had good memories about the brand, so he knew there was space in the customers' mind that a revival strategy could tap into with sharp positioning. He got the company to think of Farmtrac and Powertrac as different brands, with the former capitalising on its Ford legacy and the latter being positioned as more of a mass brand. This clarity led to changes in design as well as marketing strategy. Farmtrac and Powertrac got separate dealerships.

One of his first tasks was to draw up three priorities: money, competition-centric leadership plan, and aligning the whole organisation, in that order. Within two months of joining, Sridhar got a benchmarking study done and conducted a strategy alignment workshop. The study showed the extent of problem within the company. The sales realisation per tractor was lower than that of competitors. The material cost was close to 73 per cent of sales, 4 to 5 per cent higher than that of other companies. The manpower costs were more than 9 per cent of sales against the industry average of 6 per cent (the best was 4 per cent). The EBIDTA margin was around 7 per cent, way lower than the industry average of 14 per cent at that time. Escorts had the lowest profitability, even though it had regained third place in market share; a multinational rival with a market share in single digits made more money. The alignment workshop with the entire management team had everyone speaking frankly about the problems they faced in discharging their responsibilities.

In line with Nikhil's keenness to promote talent internally, Sridhar also identified leaders within Escorts and put them in key positions; this was a huge morale booster for the organisation. Shenu Agarwal, who was head of marketing, was made head of R&D in the Knowledge Management Centre (KMC) and later strategy added to his role; Rajneesh Agarwal was made head of design; Nijagun Hiremath was put in charge of Escorts Crop Solutions; and Ankur Gupta was made head of quality. Among those he brought in from outside, notable was Sameer Tandon as chief sales and marketing officer; he had been heading sales at Monsanto India.

He then authored a four-layered technology roadmap. The first stage, called catch-up, involved catching up with competition, doing whatever was possible given the financial constraints. Very little investment in technology had happened during Chadha's and Mal's time, for no fault of either CEO. During Chadha's time, this was because of lack of funds and the need to just get production going. During Mal's time, the focus was addressing hygiene issues and achieving a measure of financial stability. As a result, Escorts products were lagging behind those of the competition. The second layer was 'current most advanced' – endeavouring to be the best in existing levels of technology and product quality. The third was 'future most advanced' – working to be the best in technology, quality and reliability in five to seven years. The fourth was about disruption and innovation. This plan required a capex outlay of Rs 380 crore in two to three years. Rajan Nanda, who never stinted on money for technology, sanctioned it.

The first layer, which kicked off in 2012, had Shailendra, Shenu and Rajneesh working closely, looking at how they could, as quickly as possible, improve quality and bring in new features in the existing range of products. One feature that was introduced was oil-immersed brakes that lasted longer and were more effective; the entire industry was using this technology. This phase was completed in nine months. The financial position further improved and it was now possible for Escorts to move to the 'current most advanced' layer.

Gaps in the Escorts product portfolio were identified and sought to be plugged. Since this was an area where Escorts was still a bit weak, the company went in for foreign partnerships in a big way. It tied up with Italy's Agritalia on ergonomics, Austrian automotive manufacturer Magna Steyr for transmissions, Italy's MITA Oleodinamics for hydraulics and revived its old partnership with Austria's AVL for engines. New series of tractors (notably the Executive series in Farmtrac and the Euro series in Powertrac, which in 2019 were the fastest-growing tractor platforms) were launched. New products like Steeltrac, a tractor specifically designed for cotton, groundnut and vegetable farms for which normal-size tractors are not suited, and the anti-lift tractor (ALT) were introduced. Escorts entered into a manufacturing alliance with a Gujarat-based company, Adico Group, to produce Steeltrac under the Escorts brand name. The ALT technology stopped the nose of the tractor from lifting when heavy equipment or trolley was attached to the back. This was an important milestone for Escorts because it was now getting into the haulage space – till now its tractors had mainly been for farming operations, even as the use of tractors for non-agricultural purposes was increasing. Existing tractor series got improved engines and transmission systems. But this is not an exercise with a sunset clause. Though most of the work in the 'current most advanced' phase got completed by 2015, it is actually a continuous journey of new designs and improvements. The Escorts R&D team, till well into 2019, brings out new products almost every quarter.

With Sridhar setting a stiff target of doubling the EBIDTA margin in three years, Escorts got focussed on profits like never before. Fighting in the highly competitive tractor market of that time without a war chest, he used to point out, was next to impossible. An outright war on costs was waged over the next few years. The material and manpower costs were identified as the biggest drags. In July 2014, a two-year Project Shikhar was launched with a specialised consulting firm as partner. It had three objectives: rationalising material costs, rationalising the number of suppliers and reducing the inventory days. Over the two-year life-cycle of the project, the material cost was reduced to around 67 per cent of sales. Earlier, in January 2013, Total Productive Maintenance (TPM, a Japanese system focussing on zero accident, breakdown, wastage and defects) had been introduced and this went a long way in helping improve productivity and savings. India faced two years of drought in 2013-14 and 2014-15, because of which the tractor industry was in recession mode. Yet, Escorts managed to improve its margins.

To energise the whole sales and marketing network, Sridhar held fifty-two dealer meetings during the first one and a half years, explaining to dealers what changes he planned to bring in and why they were needed. Sameer Tandon then stepped up to the plate. On him fell the task of placing the farmer – the final customer – at the heart of marketing efforts, thus resetting the earlier skew towards dealers and invigorating the Escorts sales team. He brought in many new practices in managing the sales pipelines and making dealers more accountable, which made him a bit unpopular with them.

Even as the second-rung leaders were working on their various responsibilities, Nikhil Nanda and Sridhar were collaborating closely on future growth.

Sridhar decided to position Farmtrac vis-à-vis world number one John Deere – even though its market share in India was just 5 per cent – rather than market leaders Mahindra and TAFE. There were three objectives behind this. One, to sidetrack the real competition – the domestic players – who would not take this seriously since John Deere's volumes were small and it would not have responded. Sridhar drew this deception technique from Sun Tzu's *Art of War*.[1] This would give Escorts the space to prepare for the giant leap. Two, the very idea of taking on the world's number one would invigorate the organisation. Three, it would help pitch Farmtrac to consumers as a premium brand.

The fact that tractors could have an aspirational appeal was brought home to Sridhar during one of his dealer interaction trips. In Varanasi, he met a prosperous farmer with large land holdings. He had a 55 HP tractor though the soil conditions on his land did not require a large tractor. When Sridhar questioned him about his choice, the farmer, who also had a strapping physique and was locally influential, answered: '*Aap mere ko dekh rahein hain* (can't you see me?).' He was also dismissive about the tractors that multinational brands were selling – their appearance did not match his physical and social stature. That made Sridhar grasp the importance of looks in a tractor; super performance and great quality were just hygiene issues.

Armed with that knowledge, Sridhar decided to get Escorts focussed on styling, something it was not paying any attention to. In 2012, Escorts first approached Italian car design and coachbuilder firm Pininfarina,[2] which designed the Ferrari sports car, but could not get an appointment. Nikhil was stung by the snub – Escorts had partnered with the world's best through its history and here was a company that was being dismissive. Instead of the normal response of going to the next best, he upped Escorts's ambition and decided to approach Studio F.A. Porsche. The audacious move was met with scepticism, but in 2013 Escorts signed up Porsche to design a series of tractors for the European market.[3] Manufactured by Farmtrac Tractors Europe (the Poland-based subsidiary), the New Escorts Tractor Series (NETS) was unveiled at Agritechnica 2017, showcase of the global agricultural engineering industry. For Nikhil this was a vindication of sorts. Soon after signing up Porsche, he had gone to London for a roadshow. When he was making a presentation to one investment firm, he faced open scepticism – nobody thought an Indian tractor company could aim so high.

IN ORDER TO leverage the full value of these partnerships, attention needed to be paid to the production systems at home. Despite all the process improvements and alignment that Mal had brought in, Escorts tractors still did not make the cut on quality. This was brought home to Nikhil Nanda brutally when Sridhar took him to meet a customer in Bathinda, Punjab, on a cold, wintry evening in January 2014. The affluent farmer had lined up his fifteen tractors, only three of which were Escorts. The next four hours were probably the longest Nikhil had ever gone through. The farmer showed how Escorts more than paled in comparison to its competitors. The gears were difficult to move, whereas they were smooth in the others. He spoke about oil leakage, parts that just stopped working and sheet metal so thin that the whole chassis vibrated when he started the tractor. 'You want me to pay Rs 5.5 lakh for a tractor that vibrates as I drive it?' he asked. Another farmer said his tractor had been delivered with an indicatory bulb missing.

For Nikhil this was a wake-up call – literally. He hardly slept for the next four days, agonising over how HPN's company could get so disconnected from the customer. Why are we in business if this is what we are giving to the customer? Why isn't this feedback coming right into the centre of the company? Why shouldn't the managers also lose their sleep over this kind of feedback?

He then called a meeting of all the departments involved in the production and sale of tractors. It was one of the rare instances when he lost his temper. 'This is not on, this is not what Escorts is meant to be. We are getting back on our feet and we cannot afford to be blindfolded. We have to open our eyes,' he said, thumping the table angrily. From then started a systematic assault on the innumerable silos in Escorts, with a great deal of emphasis on improving internal coordination and communication, through dashboards and regular MIS reports. Taking a cue from Nikhil's unease over the organisation's disconnect with its customer, the then assistant vice-president of human resources, Charu Maini, conceptualised the Empathy programme, which had employees being required to spend one week in a village.

The trip to Bathinda was part of Nikhil's effort to engage more with all of Escorts's external stakeholders. His resolve was strengthened when, in the course of his first interaction with dealers, the owner of one of Escorts's oldest dealers came up to him. Seema Gupta, whose husband's grandfather had started the dealership in the '60s, said: '*Hum to aapke bachche hain, aap bachchon ko chhod dete hain* (We are your children, do you abandon your children like this)? When a puzzled Nikhil asked her what she meant, she said they had not met anyone from the promoter family after HPN. 'We have only heard of your father. If you don't meet us and talk to us, how will we progress?' Her tone may have seemed melodramatic but she was echoing the feeling of most dealers, especially the older ones who remembered HPN often landing up unannounced and always willing to lend an ear to their problems.

Nikhil now makes regular visits to dealers and customers, many of which are unscheduled or arranged at very short notice. It is not always possible to go incognito, but he loses no chance to either pose as a customer or get someone accompanying him to do so at the outlets of dealers.

He has brought that same approach into his interaction with suppliers, especially the smaller ones in and around Faridabad, many of whom owe their origins to Escorts. Their communication with the top management had broken down, especially during the time of turbulence when even people in the purchase department would avoid their calls when they wanted to check on payments. The annual supplier meetings have been resumed and Nikhil makes every effort to be accessible to them. Importantly, the TPM initiative was extended to the factories of some key suppliers in 2015, and the Escorts team is closely involved in hand-holding and mentoring them. The quality of Escorts tractors has started to show significant improvement.

Even as Escorts was struggling to get back into leadership position in the domestic market, Nikhil set his sights on the export market. This did seem imprudent, considering the company was still addressing issues relating to quality, but Nikhil had set his mind to it. In 2013, Escorts participated in an international exhibition – Agritechnica, at Hanover – for the first time, despite Rajan Nanda's disinclination. The Farmtrac Heritage series was put on display. It got a lot of appreciation and a year later it was rolled out in South Africa and Bangladesh. However, efforts to forge technology and marketing partnerships with European companies for global markets came to naught. Rajan and Nikhil Nanda as well as Sridhar approached Italian firm Same Duetz-Fahr and Germany's Claas for collaborations, but nothing came of this.

Escorts then approached Italian firm BCS for a design partnership. Sridhar believed that the future of tractors lay in the lightweight ones being manufactured in Korea and Japan by LS Mtron and Kubota Corporation respectively and that Escorts should start preparing to deal with this challenge. BCS offered the technology that was the closest in similarity to what LS and Kubota had. Rajan and Nikhil Nanda had several meetings with Fabrizio Castoldi, president of BCS, but the price he quoted for sharing the technology was too steep. However, Escorts got the marketing rights in India for BCS's Ferrari orchard and vineyard tractors, to explore a new opportunity area.

Nikhil was disappointed at Escorts not being able to get the technology that would have enabled it to take on global leaders in the future. He was mulling over this one day and it struck him that it might be a good idea to collaborate with Kubota instead of preparing to challenge it over time. He immediately shot off a letter to the president of Kubota, Masatoshi Kimata, suggesting that the two companies could work together. The response was positive and Nikhil met Yuichi Kitao, the director of Kubota, in Bangkok in 2013. The initial meeting went off well and for the next one and a half years there were wide-ranging discussions about the contours of a partnership. This was another issue on which father and son had major differences of opinion which got aired in front of senior executives.

Rajan Nanda had not been very comfortable with the idea of partnering with Kubota, but later agreed with two conditions – Kubota would not be given equity in Escorts and there should be a no-compete clause. The negotiations were tortuous and were spread over nearly four years. Just before leaving for Bangkok for one crucial meeting, Nikhil thought it best to brief the chairman about the agenda and the line Escorts planned to take. Rajan Nanda was unwell and at home that day, and Nikhil, Sridhar and Gaurav Malhotra, head of strategy, went across to see him. Sridhar and Malhotra started to show him the PowerPoint presentation, when he interrupted and asked who had authorised the trip and the discussion. 'You don't have my mandate,' he said, before berating all three of them. When the meeting ended, the shaken trio went to a nearby hotel for tea. Sridhar dissuaded Nikhil from going ahead with the trip because the chairman, who was also his father, was not blessing it. Nikhil, however, was firm that Escorts, which once grew with the help of partnerships, needed the tie-up with Kubota at this stage of the journey. As a son he was upset and did not want to disrespect his father, but as a professional he felt he would not be able to respect himself if he gave up the chance to give Escorts a technological leg-up.

After a sleepless night, he left the next morning for Bangkok; he hardly spoke to Sridhar and Malhotra on the plane, embarrassed by his father's outburst. The meeting went off well and while returning the same day, he called Rajan Nanda from Bangkok airport to brief him on what happened. His sense of hurt as a son could not override his duty as a professional to keep his chairman informed. He was nervous but his father was grace personified, saying he was glad the meeting went off well and that he was quite encouraged by the possibility of the two companies working together.

A week later, the talks hit a roadblock, as Kubota sought equity in Escorts. After almost a year, Shailendra Agrawal suggested starting the search for partners again. He initially proposed talks with Korea's LS Mtron. By that time, Nikhil's initiative of addressing the issue of unpaid dues from Farmtrac North America had smoothened relations between the two companies. But since negotiations with Kubota had been at an advanced stage, a decision was taken to give that partnership one last shot. Nikhil got in touch with Kubota again and discussions resumed. After extensive discussions, Escorts and Kubota entered into a joint venture in December 2018, involving both technology collaboration and joint manufacturing, with Escorts holding 40 per cent stake. Rajan Nanda had passed away a few months earlier but he had blessed the partnership while he was alive.

Under the joint venture, a common manufacturing facility with a capacity of 50,000 tractors will be set up, allowing Escorts access to Kubota technology. In essence, this will be a combination of Japanese cutting-edge technology and Indian frugal engineering. These high-end, value-oriented utility tractors will be sold by both partners domestically through their separate channels (Kubota already has a presence in the Indian market). In addition, the tractors will be co-branded as E-Kubota for sale in the export market, through Kubota's global distribution network. So, apart from technology and process excellence that the joint venture will bring for Escorts, it will also give the company an international playing field far bigger than what it could have achieved on its own, and much faster as well. This joint venture can, over time, become a game changer for Escorts.

Unfortunately, towards April 2016, Sridhar, who had kickstarted this and several other initiatives, wanted to be excused for personal reasons. By that time, the tractor division was in much sounder financial shape (the EBITDA margin had improved to 10 per cent) and great partnerships had been forged. However, market share kept declining, with Sonalika crossing Escorts in 2015-16, and that was the ultimate test for Rajan Nanda. A year earlier, one of the key members of Sridhar's team, Sameer Tandon, had been made vice-president, international business, where there was nothing much to do; he quit Escorts in March 2016. Another CEO was appointed briefly for the agri-machinery division; by this time, Nikhil started gaining confidence that he could be the CEO as well. In any case, he had other plans as far as leadership was concerned.

NIKHIL NANDA WANTED the new agri-machinery CEO to settle down, bring in the right strategic approach for the business, and take it forward from where Sridhar had left it. He requested Sridhar to be around for some six more months and supervise the agri initiatives and closely watch the developments. Sridhar was also requested to supervise the construction equipment division during this transition period and take over as CEO of the construction business, which was just emerging from four years of continuous decline. Since around 2010, the infrastructure sector – the main source of business for construction equipment – had been in near-paralysis mode and several large infrastructure projects had stalled. A new government was laying a lot of emphasis on roads and urban development and demand was expected to pick up. In 2015-16, the industry saw a 15 per cent growth, but the division was making losses.[4] Sridhar did try to bring in some insights in terms of strategy, but this was not an industry he was very familiar with. After bringing the agri business new leadership and the construction business to a fair pace, Sridhar left Escorts though he continues to be involved as a strategic consultant.

Nothing brings out the change in the perception about Escorts among professionals than the case of Ajay Mandahr, who came in as CEO of the ECE division in October 2016. Mandahr, who was operations director at Toyota Material Handling, India, had been approached by Escorts in 2012 but he was just not interested in the company, though good professionals had started joining. When approached again, he was still diffident, but Ishan Mehta, Executive Vice-President, Human Resources, asked him to meet Nikhil. When he did, Mandahr found Nikhil to be a no-nonsense person passionately committed to growing the business. He later met Rajan Nanda and found him also to be enthusiastic about the business. It was only then that he decided to take the plunge.

Within weeks of his joining, he realised he had his work cut out for him. As in the tractor division, there were watertight silos here as well – the parts, service, sales divisions were not communicating with each other. There were no processes in place. New product development was in a shambles. The after-sales service was poor, leading to customers being dissatisfied. And, because of the history of losses, employee morale was extremely low.

In his first three months, Mandahr shifted or removed general managers heading various departments. Some, like parts and services, were combined. Not only did this break the silos, it also reduced costs and improved accountability. It did cause disruption but sent out a clear message on performance.

He turned attention to boosting employee morale. By the time he joined, the integration of HR systems across businesses had already been done, as had the revamping of performance assessment. Key result areas (KRAs) had also been defined. But Mandahr was still not entirely satisfied with methods to assess performance. He arranged for a separate workshop for the ECE team on setting KRAs as well as performance assessment. This brought in more rigour into the evaluation process. People were wary, but in the last quarter of 2016-17 ECE started to show some profits. This helped in creating the impression that perhaps the new team was doing something right. Then in 2017-18, the better performers were rewarded; this not only boosted their morale but also sent out a message to the sub-par performers that good work would be recognised.

As for the division as a whole, Mandahr did not measure performance either in terms of market share or profitability. For him it was all about putting the customer at the centre of everything and designing all processes around this; both market share and profitability would follow, he believed.

The product portfolio needed a lot of attention. Mandahr found there was lack of clarity on the identity of ECE and that there was no segregation of parts either in the manufacturing or marketing stage. This was affecting product development as well. So he first pitched ECE as primarily a crane company. He then created three verticals within ECE: material handling (pick-and-carry cranes);

earth moving and compactors. This would result in specialisation within ECE.

Within the cranes portfolio, Mandahr started playing around with the product mix. The products were classified as high-value and low-value; the latter category was further segmented in terms of tonnage. Those products that were not giving good margins were to be slowly phased out, while those that were profitable were to be given more play. A similar approach was taken in the earth moving and compactor portfolios as well – a greater play for some, focussing on niche markets for others and on exports for yet others. Attention then turned to developing new products, improving on existing ones and forging new tie-ups. At the 2018 Bauma CONEXPO, an international trade fair for the construction machinery and equipment sector, ECE unveiled three new products. The significant achievement, however, was on the collaborations front.

The biggest of these tie-ups was the joint venture with Japan's Tadano group, the world's leading mobile crane manufacturer, in August 2018. Tadano Escorts, in which Escorts holds 49 per cent stake, will introduce rough terrain and truck-mounted cranes in the Indian market. In another instance of combining Japanese technology with Indian frugal engineering, it will help Escorts get an edge in the heavier-capacity cranes and cater far more effectively to construction companies servicing oil refineries, metro rail projects and smart city projects, among others.

The partnership with Kubota on tractors had a spin-off benefit for ECE as well. Its back-hoe loader will gain from a joint branding arrangement for the export market, leveraging Kubota's global distribution channel. Earlier, ECE had signed an agreement with the American subsidiary of Italian firm JMG Cranes on battery-operated self-propelled pick-and-carry cranes. This was one negotiation that Rajan Nanda had been very keen on and he had even attended some of the early meetings. ECE also bagged exclusive distribution rights in India of Korean firm Doosan Infracore, a global leader in the construction equipment sector.

Mandahr realised that rolling out new products would help only up to a point. Products needed to be sold and serviced; ECE was weak in both these areas.

Attention was first turned to toning up the dealer network, which was in a shambles because of the recession in the industry. As in the case of tractors, ECE also had a dealer-centric model, where dealers pushed sales and ECE gave them a commission. Mandahr changed that model. Now ECE sales people had to go out into the field and sell equipment. The orders were routed through the dealers, who got a commission to help them revive, but the primary responsibility was that of the ECE staff.

Dealers were also found to be slightly tardy in providing after-sales support. A call centre was set up and a toll-free number printed on every machine in a way that it was visible to both customers and dealers. The complaints that came in were analysed and their resolution monitored. One problem identified was that of parts management. It was found that the first fill (the number of items that can be picked in one go once an order is received) was a low 35 per cent in 2017. A parts warehouse was set up and processes put in place which improved the first fill to 77 per cent within two years. This helped improve the credibility of the after-sales service. The manner of penalising dealers who do not give good after-sales support also changed – earlier their territories were pared down; now non-performing dealers are just replaced. It has become clear to dealers now that providing after-sales support is a crucial parameter of performance, which it was not earlier.

Within ECE, all the complaints that come in are collated and a root cause analysis carried out. Suitable corrective action is taken where needed on the product development or sales and marketing or service side. The feedback loop is not one-sided from the customer's end. Cross-functional teams comprising R&D, sales, service, production and quality go to the customers and ask them about problems they face. A human touch campaign was launched for a brief period, as part of which select ECE employees were each given the task of calling a particular customer and getting feedback on the product.

One difficult task was to get money that was stuck in the market. Again, just like the tractor division, ECE also worked on the basis of giving credit to dealers, but getting money back was proving to be a problem. A 6X6X6 campaign was launched – Rs 6 crore from six dealers in six months. That helped to some extent but the problem of collection has not been decisively overcome. However, the combined effect of all these actions was an improvement in the financial position of the division. It clocked a positive EBIT in the fourth quarter of 2016-17 – for the first time after twenty-two quarters. The EBIT was still negative for the whole year, but the extent of the loss was lower after nearly six years.

THE RAILWAY EQUIPMENT business was the smallest in the Escorts portfolio but had always been a profitable one – its EBITDA margins, though low, had always been in the positive zone. However, it was not performing up to its potential, and it, too, was going through a CEO churn since 2007; in 2012-13, the EBIT was down to 8.5 per cent and the following year 9.5 per cent. Dipankar Ghosh was brought in as business head in October 2012. A former Indian Railway Service officer, he had also worked in R&D with Bombardier and Caterpillar. Rajan Nanda, while interviewing him, very frankly admitted that Escorts did not have the systems and processes he was used to in multinational companies. It was this frankness that led Ghosh to decide on taking up the assignment.

Ghosh found Rajan Nanda had not been exaggerating. He landed in a situation where processes, whether financial or operational, existed only on paper. There was no proper assessment of the cost of materials. There was some desultory bargaining with suppliers, but no attempt to understand how the cost was arrived at. He also found that a large percentage of the products of the railway equipment division were on the verge of extinction.

Ghosh first set about putting systems and processes in place, working along with an internal audit team. He had to fire a few people, because he did not think they would fit into the process-driven environment he was planning to put in place. Some of them had been with the company for more than twenty years and it showed a huge change within Escorts that he was allowed to let them go within a few months of his joining.

He then embarked on an ambitious project of new product development, bringing in three people from Bombardier, including the head of R&D. Over the next few years he managed to successfully woo close to seventy-five people into the division, including people who were working in Europe with Bombardier and Alstom. These new executives drove the expansion of the product portfolio, with several high-end products, which only multinational companies were supplying earlier. Typically, in the railways sector, new products have a long go-to-market period because of the rigorous testing requirements. Many of these products started coming into the market from 2018 and the frugal engineering adopted in Escorts has meant that many of these products are nearly half the price of that of foreign companies. What has also worked for Escorts is that the R&D is done here, unlike in the case of many multinationals whose centre of excellence is in their home countries. Escorts, therefore, has a faster response time, which has given it an edge. Apart from developing new products, the people Ghosh brought in were also managing to tweak existing products and manage a great deal of cost optimisation, which increased the value of these products and, hence, demand.

Importantly, their knowledge of products made negotiations with suppliers more rigorous. Far more detailed questions were now asked of suppliers and they could not fob off these experts with vague answers. This, along with getting alternative suppliers for some components, resulted in a significant increase in margins.

Ghosh then set his sights on the export market. This was prompted by a monthly update that Nikhil circulates on the performance of all the divisions on various parameters. This generates a competitive spirit within the organisation and that worked in the case of the railways division. In these updates, the railway division was found to be underperforming. Ghosh decided to do something about it. He found that Africa, which used to be a significant market, had dropped out. It turned out that the African countries were sourcing from China. Escorts then went and pitched in China, offering to make brake systems for the African market at a price that was significantly lower. Escorts bagged the order in 2018 and, within six months, had shipped 1,200 sets.

Soon the profitability of the division started to improve and this not only boosted the morale of the employees, but also increased the trust the promoters had in Ghosh's leadership. So when Ghosh asked for one more factory, they were quick to give the green signal.

The compound in which the railway equipment division is located was also home to two factories of the tractor division – one produced spare parts and the other crankshafts. The crankshaft factory was under-utilised while the railway equipment division had seen turnover increase by three times and was still growing. Ghosh, therefore, asked for this plant, only to be met with stiff resistance within Escorts. He then threw down a challenge. The crankshaft plant had an annual turnover of Rs 50 crore; he said he would push the plant's turnover to Rs 350 crore in three years. Nikhil warned him that he would hold him to the promise. The factory was handed over in 2017. The union gave Ghosh and his employee relations manager a hard time but they managed to win them over. When he visited the factory six months later, Nikhil was surprised to see how it had been transformed with minimal expenditure.

By 2019, the division was clocking EBIT margin of upwards of 20 per cent, something it could only dream of at one point of time. Like the other divisions, it was also inking collaborations with global majors. One of them was a technical collaboration agreement with South Korean firm Yujin Machinery for sophisticated brake systems for high-speed trains and rolling stock. More importantly, it was making a name for itself for frugal engineering, so it started to be chased instead of it chasing business. Indian Railways reached out to it to develop doors and other products for it. European companies also started approaching it for collaborations. One of them was Germany's Bode AG, which approached it to manufacture doors for metro trains. Nikhil Nanda often tells Ghosh that he should grow the railway equipment business to a level at which Escorts can add the tag line: 'We also make tractors.'[5]

THERE WAS ONE business which defied all attempts to breathe life into it – Escorts Auto Products (EAP) division. It had not been able to move out of the red for over fifteen years, despite efforts by various CEOs. After the tractor division, this was the closest to Rajan Nanda's heart, since he had started his career in the company with this division. This was another business where Escorts used to have a strong presence but had not been able to sustain it in the keenly competitive post-liberalisation scenario.

Around 2009, plans were drawn up to get the division to start catering more to the four-wheeler industry and to redefine the business model by, among other things, extending the Escorts brand for everyday consumables like brake products, grease and oil, exhausts. But that did not help. Ghosh was given additional charge of EAP in 2014, after the then CEO left. He was told to see if he could revive the division. But that was a bad time for the auto industry – it had been getting by because of the excise duty cuts that were part of the stimulus package the government had announced at the time of the global financial crisis in 2008. The division's top three original equipment manufacturer (OEM) customers had, for over a year, reported a decline in production in the range of 15 per cent to 25 per cent.

Ghosh tried his best. EAP increased its presence in the aftermarkets both at home and abroad, expanding its footprint to more countries. New products were developed for OEM customers as well as high margin exports and the aftermarkets. He also focussed on cutting the fixed and semi-variable costs. All this did not help very much – EBIT losses declined but were still substantial. Meanwhile, the investor community would ask questions about this at every interaction with the company; it believed this was detracting from Escorts's intrinsic value and could not understand why Escorts was continuing in a business with no possibility of growth. Making the business a robust one would have required very large investment and the margins were too thin to warrant that. Shutting it down or selling it off seemed the only sensible option. Ghosh took one division of EAP that was supplying parts to the railways and integrated it with the railway equipments division.

The problem was that EAP had over 350 workers, which was not only unsustainable for the business but would have also put off buyers. Ghosh had been assured that he could do whatever he wanted to downsize it. That brought him up against the union. It took months of negotiating, sometimes into the wee hours, with Ghosh and the human resources team explaining that the business could not be run with such huge manpower, and if it could not be run, job losses would be inevitable. Finally the union agreed to a voluntary retirement scheme (VRS) for the whole group and this brought the worker headcount at EAP down to around eighty.

Rajan Nanda just could not bring himself to agree to sell, not even when Nikhil told him that Escorts had lost Rs 100 crore over five years because of it. He then suggested that the business be restructured and operations shifted to the EAP plant in Rudrapur in Uttarakhand; he said he would allocate Rs 30 crore for this. Nikhil, however, pointed out that moving geography is not a business plan; the company would spend another Rs 30 crore on shifting it, but the division would still be making losses. It took Rajan Nanda several weeks to come around. Finally on 11 August 2016, EAP was sold to Pune-based Badve Engineering for around Rs 17 crore.

The most startling part of the sale was the market reaction to it – that day the Escorts scrip crossed the upper circuit by 20 per cent. Nikhil was surprised at the significance for shareholders of selling such a small unit. It was then that he understood why Shrikant Badve, managing director of Badve Engineering, had told him during the negotiations: 'Why are you worried about Rs 1 crore or Rs 2 crore that Escorts will get or not get. The change in perception and rise in share price that you will get after the sale will be much, much more.' A year before the sale, Nikhil had walked into an investor meeting at one of the plants with all the CEOs. He was asked about his plans for EAP. He said that Escorts did not plan to be in the business in the long run. For the investment community, the sale of EAP was a turning point; it showed that the top management was now delivering on its guidance (the group's reputation on this had been a bit tarnished earlier) and that it was now determined to concentrate its energies on its core businesses. This investor interest was also of relatively recent origin.

SOME TIME IN 2015, Chintan Modi, a mid-cap analyst with Motilal Oswal, was running screeners on a database of all listed companies looking for, one, a turnaround story and, two, something interesting happening in companies in the agriculture-related space (the monsoon outlook was good, after two back-to-back drought years). Among the companies that the screener threw up, one was Escorts. When he looked more closely, he found the initial data interesting. He got in touch with Prateek Singhal of Escorts's investor relations team, who set up more interactions within the company. Modi was pleasantly surprised at what he learnt.

So was another analyst who had been tracking the tractor industry since 2005. Escorts had not been on his radar because it was not among the large-cap stocks. While interacting with dealers across states in 2015, he and his team learnt that interesting things were happening in Escorts – it was coming out with new products, plugging product gaps and improving quality.

Why had a once blue-chip company gone off the radar of the investor community? An analyst following the company since 2012 found that it had not been able to leverage the potential of the brand. From a markets perspective, the valuations were always cheap because of the returns it used to deliver on the balance sheet. And then there was a lot of churn in the management, because of which investors were worried about the long-term strategy of the company.

There was, he recalls, speculation about whether the promoters were even interested in the business.

It was only in 2009, during Mal's time, that a dedicated investor cell was set up. This was part of an overall restructuring of the finance department in which specific cells for treasury, banking and investors were set up within the department. However, there were no regular conference calls or meetings with analysts – an important tool for them to get a sense of a company's ability to deliver and, on that basis, recommend a stock. But the company had started doing well and it had an institutional holding of around 47 per cent in 2010-11, of which 31 per cent was held by foreign institutional investors (FIIs). Unfortunately, the CFO, who had not been in touch with the heads of various businesses, had made over-optimistic commitments on performance which were not met. The tractor industry was hit by drought and Escorts's volumes and revenues fell, the share price plummeted to the Rs 40-50 range. Angry investors blamed the management for deliberately misleading them and there was heavy selling of the company stock. Institutional holding came down to 10 per cent in 2013-14. At a time when the company should have been engaging with investors, it went into a shell for close to six months; the investor cell had, in any case, closed since all members of the team had moved out.

In 2013, the investor relations function was outsourced to an agency and, encouraged by Madan (who was now CFO), it started getting the Escorts management, including Rajan and Nikhil Nanda, to interact more closely with analysts and investors. The turning point came in August 2013 when Nikhil, along with Sridhar, Madan and G.V. Murthy, the then CEO of ECE, went to Mumbai for an investor conference. They met some other institutional investors as well, one of whom read them the riot act. He told Sridhar: 'Last time your managing director came with another set of CEOs and promised 100 steps; not one was done.' Sridhar just asked him to put Escorts on his radar and not buy any stock for now. That financial institution later became one of the large shareholders in Escorts.

During various roadshows and interactions with investors and stakeholders, Escorts also happened to meet Rakesh Jhunjhunwala. In his extremely soft tone, Mr Jhunjhunwala first grilled Sridhar and then the rest of the team. Nikhil Nanda was also not spared. Mr Jhunjhunwala knew about Sridhar's work and felt that professionals like him would not join a company unless it was a good story. He then looked at the Escorts balance sheet and found very little downside in the stock.

Mr Jhunjhunwala recalls that Nikhil Nanda made a very emotional appeal – I come from a proud lineage and I want to prove something. At a time when everyone was sceptical of Escorts and the Nandas, Mr Jhunjhunwala believed him.

Intuition, he says, plays a big role in investment decisions and he could see that Nikhil Nanda was genuinely sincere. After one and a half hours of interaction, he took Nikhil Nanda aside and said: 'I see the hunger in your eyes, I love the story you have conveyed, I am convinced.' Subsequently, it was informed that Mr Jhunjhunwala did buy the stock the very next morning, which went a long way in changing the perception of Escorts in the markets and interest perked up.

It was not just the perception of investors which changed, Escorts also realised it needed to change the way it engaged with the markets. Before 2012, analysts had to be content with interacting only with the CFOs of individual businesses; they did not meet the CEOs, let alone Rajan or Nikhil Nanda. When analysts started seriously tracking the company, they made it clear to Singhal that they wanted to meet the CEOs. Madan, who was group CFO, readily agreed and started facilitating these interactions. Regular plant visits helped the analysts get a more realistic picture. Not only did the number of interactions with the top management increase, analysts also found the quality of the interactions improving. Nikhil Nanda made himself accessible. Transparency increased and the guidance by the top management became more realistic. What struck Mitul Shah of Reliance Securities was the clarity of the management about where things had gone wrong and their strategy to deal with this.

This change in the way Escorts was perceived had to be extended to the wider world. It was now time for an image makeover.

ON THE WALL of the foyer leading to Nikhil Nanda's office, there are framed articles and reports that have appeared in the media about Escorts. Till about 2015, it was blank, with just a photo of HPN there. From around the time Mal left, Escorts had more or less dropped out of the media radar, barring a few interviews with Nikhil after he became managing director and occasional articles following the tie-up with Ferrari. There were only one or two articles on the revival he was attempting. He also realised that communication channels within the company were blocked. He needed to do something on both fronts.

Some time in 2014, the co-author of this book, Sharad Gupta, who was then heading marketing and brand strategy for Xerox India and South Asia, got a message over LinkedIn from Praveen Sinha of the HR department. That led to a conversation over coffee with Ishan Mehta. Mehta told him the company was looking for someone to take care of brand communication and marketing. A few days later, even as Gupta was mulling over this, he was invited to meet Nikhil. At the meeting, Nikhil was upfront – Escorts' communication, branding and marketing push was not delivering results and he needed some fresh thinking. When, after a couple of weeks, Gupta said he was ready to come on board, he was invited to meet Rajan Nanda, who told him about how Escorts was an institution more than a brand and how he wanted to take it to greater heights.

When he finally joined, Gupta realised he would have his hands full. Escorts, once famous as a premier engineering company, was now known only as a tractor and hospital company. In the mind of the general public, it was still associated with the hospital business, even though that had been sold a decade back. It was not just about the media and the public – Escorts was also disconnected from industry associations and trade bodies like the Confederation of Indian Industry (CII), Federation of Indian Chambers of Commerce and Industry (FICCI) – two chambers where HPN had been very active. As a result, Escorts did not have the right forums at which to engage with policy makers. The agency that handled the company's media relations found it difficult to pitch stories to the press. When someone did bite the bait and wanted to interview Nikhil, he tended to demur. For close to a decade, there had been no strong marketing push – the last was in 2003 when actors Amitabh Bachchan, who was also Nikhil's father-in-law, and Sunny Deol were appointed brand ambassadors. The brand's Klout score (Klout is an online tool that measures social media influence) was an abysmal three. Importantly, barring Nikhil, hardly anyone in the company seemed to acknowledge that this was a problem and one that needed to be addressed urgently.

Gupta's first priority was to change this mindset. He told Rajan and Nikhil Nanda that the brand needed to talk and that the media would start getting interested in it only when it realised there was a compelling story that was waiting to be told. When he joined, he had sent out feelers to journalists to write about Escorts but got a lukewarm response. He had then decided to become more aggressive. The best way to do it was to launch a brand communication campaign.

The campaign, 'Engineering the Fundamentals of Growth', was meant to revive the image of Escorts as an engineering company. It was to cover television, print and digital platforms. The Rs 6 crore budget was considered extremely steep – the brand-building budget used to be Rs 80-90 lakh – but Nikhil realised the importance of the campaign and gave the go-ahead.

When Gupta and Nikhil went to show the final campaign to Rajan Nanda, the chairman rejected it. Escorts, he said, had never done this nor was this the right time. Nikhil told him that something like this was needed and should be allowed, but all he got was an emphatic 'No, Nikhil'. Staring at the possibility of his first big assignment collapsing, a desperate Gupta launched into a long explanation about how such a campaign was necessary and how Escorts would never be able to influence public opinion without it. After hearing him out, Rajan Nanda told Nikhil: 'I am approving it just for this young man's passion. Don't come back to me if it fails.' Relieved, Gupta got the agency to tweak it, based on suggestions from Sridhar and others in the group.

The commercial first appeared on business channel CNBC-TV18 at 9.15 a.m. on 25 May 2015. Screens were put up all over Escorts for people to see it. When they did, many employees choked with emotion – the lack of a brand identity had been getting to them too. Rajan Nanda was extremely pleased. This became a turning point. Soon journalists were putting in requests for interviews and assistance on stories. In-depth stories charting the changes within Escorts started appearing in the mainstream media. As the financial performance of the company improved, the media started taking more interest and Madan soon became a regular face on business news channels at the time of quarterly results. CEOs like Ghosh and Sridhar also started to give sound bytes regularly. From a point where top executives stayed away from interview requests to avoid embarrassing questions, CEOs now started relationship meetings with journalists. Escorts had come a long way from the time when Nikhil and Mal had gone to talk to journalists in the Mumbai office of a top financial daily; they had met with crushing scepticism.

Gupta then focussed heavily on branding. He wrote to CII outlining the brand's relevance, he started getting Rajan Nanda to attend the annual general meetings, he made Escorts get membership of CII's regional and state councils, as well as the Punjab, Haryana, Delhi Chambers of Commerce and Industry (PHDCCI), All India Management Association, Indian Marketing Association and the Faridabad Industries Association. Escorts managers across hierarchies were prodded to attend meetings of these chambers and associations. He also got Rajan Nanda to become more visible by regularly talking to the electronic media on the industry outlook till, in 2016, the chairman told him to put Nikhil out more. Nikhil was also prodded to blog regularly and make his presence felt on social media.

Next up were meetings with farmers' bodies and collaborating on programmes on the DD Kisan channel, which the public broadcaster Doordarshan had launched in 2015. When the ALT tractor was launched in 2015, one piece was placed outside Terminal 1D of Delhi's Indira Gandhi International Airport. The bright yellow tractor attracted a lot of attention, with people taking selfies and posting them on online platforms. There was scepticism within the company about whether this move would help in sales, but for Gupta that was less of a concern – he wanted Escorts to become a talking point and it had.

But perhaps the most audacious move was to do tertiary advertising through films. Raj Kapoor had used the Rajdoot motorcycle in his film *Bobby* and this made the bike a rage among the youth in the '70s. Product placement of a bike is one thing, a tractor quite another. Farmtrac made its debut in the Salman Khan starrer *Sultan.* This was built upon by having Khan star in an advertisement saying: *Sattar saalon se khet ka sultan: Escorts* (the sultan of farms for seventy years: Escorts). For the first day, first show of *Sultan*, Satyam cinema in Delhi's Nehru Place was blocked for the Escorts top management and their families. The entire Nanda family was present. The theatre was decorated with Escorts banners. This was replicated in theatres across Faridabad, and 1,500 employees, wearing Escorts T-shirts and caps, took their families to see the film. At Satyam Cineplex, Rajan Nanda called Gupta when the film ended and hugged him. Nikhil, who always craved his father's approval at work, was ecstatic when he saw this. The effect on Escorts employees was amazing – they danced in the aisles when the scene of Khan driving a Farmtrac played out. They always had an emotional connect with the company, but had been unhappy during its bad phase; it was now something they could be proud of.

Gupta had not forgotten the second part of his brief – strengthen internal communication. That, Nikhil believed, was the only way to break the silos that existed in the company and also boost employee morale. A slew of initiatives were aggressively taken. Town hall events – Connect with Nikhil – which tended to be random were made fortnightly events. Every month, good performers in each department, selected by the department heads, were invited to Coffee with Nikhil. Change agents and high performers among the blue-collar workers were invited to meet both Rajan and Nikhil Nanda once a quarter. A monthly communiqué started going out from Nikhil on the state of Escorts – turnover, profitability and other parameters. In the plants, this communiqué was read out by the plant head at the start of each shift. The knitting of Escorts into one cohesive organisation had begun.

CHAPTER SEVEN

BECOMING A FRIEND OF THE FARMERS

ON A SLIGHTLY warm September afternoon in 2018, Nikhil Nanda sat on a charpoi in a farmer's house in Dhatur village of Haryana's Palwal district. The village is known to be a captive market for one of Escorts's competitors. Three hours earlier, as he was about to set off from his office, he had told the service engineer accompanying him to take him to a non-Escorts area: 'I want to meet only non-Escorts customers or Escorts customers who are unhappy with us.'

Introducing himself as part of the sales team of Escorts, Nikhil asked the farmer why he does not own an Escorts tractor. The farmer told him he had visited a sales camp Escorts had held a year earlier because he was interested in buying a Powertrac Euro 50. The Escorts team at the camp quoted Rs 1.8 lakh as exchange price for his old tractor. But when he went to the dealer's outlet a few days later, he was told the exchange price would be only Rs 1.6 lakh. In addition, the price quoted for the Euro 50 was Rs 30,000 higher than what was mentioned in the text he had got from the Escorts sales team. The dealer was very brusque when he questioned him about these discrepancies. On the other hand, the experience with another company, he said, was very different. The dealer was extremely courteous and he bought a tractor from him, even though he also gave him only Rs 1.6 lakh for the old tractor. 'It was not about the money, but the way your dealer behaved,' he says.

Nikhil folded his hands and said: 'Dealer *ne aap se theek bartaav nahin kiya, uske liye mein haath jod kar maafi maangta hoon* (I apologise with folded hands for the behaviour of the dealer).' He then offered to give the farmer the exchange price he wanted for the other tractor he bought and to sell him a Euro 50 at the price Escorts had originally quoted. When the farmer demurred, saying he would have to adjust the implements attached to the new tractor, the Escorts team offered to provide the attachments at a nominal extra cost. He agreed. A week later, he was invited to the Escorts corporate office where Nikhil handed over the key to a Euro 50.

But this was not about Nikhil scoring PR points. On the way back to office, he was busy shooting off instructions either on WhatsApp or to the executives accompanying him scheduling an immediate meeting of the sales, production and quality teams to discuss the quality problems that farmers had pointed out and getting a showcause notice issued to the dealer the farmer complained about.

For old Escorts watchers, this was a restoration of the legacy of HPN. In the '80s, HPN once decided, on the spur of the moment, to visit some farmers on the outskirts of Delhi. Stopping at one farm, he took a sip of the offered lassi and asked why the farmer was not using his Escorts tractor. The farmer complained that the downtime was too high because spares were not easily available; he had gone to the spare parts dealer's shop at Kashmiri Gate (a hub for auto spare parts in Delhi), and was told parts were not available. HPN then drove all the way to Kashmiri Gate, some 30 km away, walked into the shop and inspected the store, grilling the storekeeper about why certain spares were not available and why there were so few of others.

Rajan Nanda's reluctance to engage with the outside world had resulted in this connect getting lost. It was only in 2011 that Sridhar started to restore the connect with both customers and dealers. It was not that the earlier CEOs did not realise the importance of this; but they had their hands more than full with fire-fighting on the financial and processes fronts to devote quality time to this. Sridhar also brought in a change in emphasis from the dealer-centric model that Escorts had to a customer-focussed one. He believed that dealers were a crucial part of the sales chain but that it was more important to connect directly with the customer.

Sridhar also brought in much-needed clarity on branding and strategy. His decision to position Farmtrac and Powertrac differently and have separate dealerships gave Escorts a major boost. In 1982, there had been a similar move by Rajan Nanda, when the Escorts tractor was segmented into Greyline and Whiteline. But there was no attempt to differentiate them as brands. Dealers also rose in revolt and the plan had then been nixed.

Nikhil has started bi-monthly visits to farmers on Sridhar's prodding. He usually tries to reach the farmer between 6 and 7 a.m. – the time farmers usually start work. That is also the thought behind the Shubharambh initiative, which has field executives reaching farms at the break of dawn. Farmers are pleased to see company staff taking this trouble and become more amenable to conversation, talking about what they think of the Escorts brand vis-à-vis competing brands and the problems they face with Escorts tractors, if they happen to own one, as well as listening to the sales pitch. This interaction is not just a one-way street, with Escorts going out to meet customers; customers are also invited to visit the factory and given conducted tours. This gives them a sense of the quality controls and processes in place to ensure that they get tractors of good quality. For Nikhil, this as well as other initiatives that would address all of a farmer's needs beyond tractors was about making Escorts a friend of the farmer.

BECOMING A FRIEND of the farmer was not entirely possible without becoming a friend of the channel partners – the dealers. The relationship between Escorts and its dealers used to be a symbiotic one during HPN's time. The head of marketing of that era, Madan Agarwal, would book trunk calls every morning at 6 to at least five dealers, making small talk and asking after their professional and personal matters. It is those memories that have seen some dealerships continue over three generations. During the Swraj Paul takeover battle, some dealers assisted the company financially. Institutions like EDDAL strengthened the bond. In Satna town of Madhya Pradesh, a roundabout in the centre of town is called Escorts Square, and in Malkanpur in Maharashtra, the village post office is called the Escorts Nagar post office after the dealership of that area. Agarwal Tractors in Satna now does business with other automobile companies but still has a model of an Escorts tractor on top of the building.

Apart from Rajan Nanda's aloofness, another reason for the relationship becoming strained in the 2000s was the slowdown in the tractor industry and Escorts's own financial constraints. Escorts leant on the dealer network to help it out of the crunch when banks and financial institutions refused to lend to it. Agarwal Automobiles in Varanasi and Rajasthan Tractor Machinery in Alwar (both of which have been dealers since the '60s) were among those who became stockists – Escorts would park tractors with them and get paid upfront while they would recoup the money when they sold further to other dealers. There were instances of dealers mortgaging their own land to get cash credit limits from banks in order to lend to Escorts. Dealers like Bimal Agarwal, founder–proprietor of Agarwal

Automobiles, and Seema Gupta of Rajasthan Tractor Machinery found nothing amiss with this – they were part of the Escorts family and this needed to be done. However, some other large dealers moved away when their inventory rose because of tractors remaining unsold and they themselves faced a financial crunch. Among them was one in Punjab which had won the best dealer award for three consecutive years. What added to their woes was lack of new products and the poor quality of tractors being rolled out of Escorts factories, which resulted in their having to face the ire of customers.

The frequent change of CEOs after Rakesh Chopra's exit had left dealers confused. By the time they adjusted to the style and projects of one CEO, they would have to deal with someone altogether different. New models and variants of tractors were introduced, which dealers would promote, and just as demand for them picked up they would be discontinued. Not only did it affect the credibility of dealers among customers, it also left them with dead stock of spare parts. This affected morale and also made them sullen and difficult.

So Sridhar and his team had to adopt a two-pronged approach to dealers – raise morale and make them more accountable.

Among the first things Tandon did was to convene a dealers' meeting. There he spoke frankly, sharing the company's strategy and action plan for the next two years. He told them that they and Escorts would have to work jointly over the next two years to be individually profitable – that they should not expect Escorts to bail them out if they were not making money. He acknowledged that Escorts had not been holding up its end of the stick, in terms of new products or good quality. That, he assured, was going to change and Escorts needed their full support for two years. All that Escorts did in the catch-up phase – fixing recurring problems in tractors, adding new features – convinced dealers that things were, indeed, going to change. There was also a clear roadmap drawn to increase prices of the high-selling models and stop the leakage of discounts on models which had strong brand recall and would have sold anyway.

Tandon then set about identifying and removing under-performing and financially unstable dealers. Over the next two years, close to 300 dealers were changed and about 300 brought into the channel finance programme, which resulted in the much-needed inflow of working capital for dealers as well as Escorts. This also increased the profitability of dealers, who otherwise were dependent on working capital at much higher interest costs. Some of the dealers who were replaced were old ones who had diversified into other businesses or dealerships because the Escorts one was no longer lucrative and not giving the company their best. Some of them were found to be taking credit from Escorts (the dealer model works heavily on credit) to finance their other businesses. There were some younger dealerships that had been brought on board without proper vetting during the time Escorts was dealing with the financial crunch. Many of these did not have the required infrastructure or proper service centres. They were dispensable because they would do more harm to the brand than bring in business. Changing dealerships was not easy, given Escorts's troubled recent history and rumours that it may close down or be sold. Some older and larger dealers appealed to Rajan Nanda, while others who were politically influential got pressure put on him indirectly. Fortunately, Nikhil backed Tandon fully.

In some areas, Escorts could not get any dealers because it had changed them quite frequently. In those areas, Tandon launched Escorts Tractor Care, a chain of service workshops which would service and repair all brands of tractors. The idea was to recoup Escorts's reputation by establishing it as a service companion for farmers and simultaneously push the brand. Modelled on the lines of Maruti Authorised Service Stations (MASS), Escorts Tractor Care had the company persuading a reputed mechanic in a particular area to invest a small sum in doing up his workshop and then training him, giving him some tools and doing some rudimentary branding. Escorts Tractor Care started with twenty outlets in 2013 and, by 2015, had 200 centres. However, this alternative servicing model led to some resentment among dealers, who saw these mechanics as competition for their own service business.

So in 2017, Shenu Agarwal, who had become the chief executive of the tractor business, changed the business model. Now Escorts identifies areas where it feels such a service is needed. It first offers the business to the local Escorts dealer; if he agrees, the centre becomes like a branch of his own outlet, albeit a multi-brand servicing centre. If he is not interested, he is asked to recommend a mechanic whom Escorts then approaches. The mechanic is trained and given help in setting up the outlet, which has Escorts signages. This arrangement is a win-win for everyone. The mechanic-owners feel this is one step in the journey to becoming dealers. There are two benefits for dealers. One, it supplements their service business (helping in areas where they are not able to send their own service teams). Two, Escorts Tractor Care customers making enquiries about Escorts tractors are directed to the dealers by the mechanic-owner; some of these enquiries get converted into sales. The customers are also pleased by the ambience of the centres and the quality of service. So for Escorts it means more business as well as higher brand equity. As of 2019, there are over 300 such outlets under this new business model alone; only a few of the 200 under the old model remain.

It was also important to institutionalise and improve upon processes to manage leads, sales and complaints. Escorts had such systems in the past, but they had fallen into disuse. One of them was SPADE (sales prospecting and demand enlistment), which involved noting down details of every enquiry and following up. Then there was SOLD (status of loan disbursement) to keep tabs on credit given to dealers. Later, when Rakesh Chopra had hired a leading consultancy firm to work out a marketing strategy, two initiatives were taken: Mission Leadership (MISSILE) and Agri Network Initiative (AGNI). Under MISSILE, data on tractor ownership was plotted on the map of a particular district to get a sense of coverage of areas by different companies. Based on this, the sales team would fan out across the district to understand why a competitor's tractor was more popular in a particular area, even if the Escorts tractor was cheaper. AGNI was a balance scorecard system for dealers, where they were rated on various parameters like showroom management, aftersales service and manpower. These had become victims of the financial crunch and it was clear that they needed to be revived, at least in spirit if not in letter.

Tandon wanted some tools that would bring dealers and Escorts on the same platform for customer relationship management. There was no way of keeping track of customer complaints about tractors, the time taken to resolve them and the reasons for any delays and whether some were repeated complaints, which would indicate the need to inform the production team.

A CRM tool was then designed, which dealers were made part of. The tool had various modules, from managing enquiries to stock position, financing and warranty claims. Some modules like warranty claims and lead management were mandatory, others were voluntary. Dealers were given an Escorts email id so that they felt part of the company. Dealers resisted this initially, but later came around when they saw that time taken for warranty claims to be settled was being scythed from six months to just about a month. A tele-marketing initiative for managing leads was also started.

Tandon, however, could not stay with these initiatives; he was transferred to the international business division in late 2015 and Shenu Agarwal took his place. He travelled across the country, meeting small groups of dealers and, later, larger groups. His father used to be a dealer of Escorts tractors in Kurukshetra and that gave him an insight into their problems, a point he often mentioned in his interactions. Some of the sessions used to last for three hours.

Shenu Agarwal initiated the Escorts Sales Management System (ESMS), which records every enquiry that is received. There is also a mobile app that is part of ESMS and all enquiries are sent as a message to the smartphone of dealer sales executives (DSEs). This becomes a daily follow-up plan for DSEs and the chances of forgetting about an older enquiry are slim. ESMS involves a regular review system at various levels. Area business managers conduct daily reviews with the four dealers that each is in charge of. Each dealer has a daily review with his DSE. Every week, the area business managers and dealers have a review session with the DSEs. And every month, the area business manager arranges for training on a specific issue. This is done by the Escorts Academy, which was set up at Plant 1 in Faridabad. Modules have been created on tactical and strategic sales moves. On the third working day of every month, DSEs are trained on a chosen module through a distance learning app called EStar or video telecast. For example, DSEs will be trained on how to approach farmers during the shraddh period (a time when it is considered inauspicious to buy new goods) and get orders which can be converted into sales and deliveries once the period is over. They are taught to visit the villages during bhajan sessions or meet the sarpanch and then take things forward from there.

Under a Mission Vijay that Shenu Agarwal started in 2015 to accelerate sales, a campaign called 'Har Gaon Dastak, Har Gaon Escorts' (knocking on every village, Escorts in every village) was launched. In this, every DSE has to spend twelve days a month, covering three villages a day. The route plan for thirty-six villages is charted out in advance. The first village is categorised as a high-priority/seeding village, where no Escorts tractor has been sold for three years. The second and third villages are visited for penetration. As part of Mission Vijay, a call centre has been set up from where calls go out to customers to verify claims made by dealers about sales, deliveries or complaints. This step corrects the pro-dealer skew that is inevitable in rural markets and connects the company directly with the customer.

What dealers are particularly happy about is the changed incentives scheme, especially the increased transparency. Rohtash Mal had brought in a number of incentive schemes which made the dealers happy. However, they were never clear about why they had, or had not, got incentives or got less than what they were expecting. Now, under the new system, detailed incentive sheets are automatically mailed to dealers every month. This gives them clarity about the calculation and allows them to work on their weak areas. From 2018, a new rating system, Escostar, was introduced. It is wider in scope than the balance scorecard that AGNI was and takes into account the entire record of enquiry generation and follow-up at dealerships as well as their inventories.

Since the tractor business is highly capital intensive, dealers often demanded credit from manufacturers. Escorts, like other tractor companies, used to arrange for channel finance from banks or get into a bill discounting arrangement. But these arrangements were backed entirely by Escorts – if the dealer defaulted, the company would have to pay the banks. Sridhar started the system of inventory financing, in which dealers would deposit collateral with the bank. The only role of Escorts was to negotiate with banks for a good rate for its dealers; after that, repayment and default was between banks and the dealers.

In 2017, a new incentive scheme called the CMD Club was started. Fifty top performing dealers are chosen to be members of this club every year, of whom eleven become members of the even more exclusive Chairman's Club. They, along with their spouses, are invited to an annual conference (different from the usual annual conferences of dealers) which revolves around a theme and at which leaders from different fields speak about how they came to the top. They then get a chance to interact on a one-to-one basis with these speakers.

Shenu Agarwal also revived EDDAL, another legacy of the HPN era that had fallen by the wayside because of the financial crunch. EDDAL, a cooperative of dealers and Escorts, had tractor dealers putting in a fixed amount for every sale. The corpus that was created was used to give soft loans to dealers, train them and their staff as well as provide insurance for salesmen and mechanics. It also used to help them set up their outlets with the right façade and infrastructure. EDDAL does much the same now. An intense ten-day training programme was organised in 2014 to train 3,000 DSEs (who are ranked silver, gold and diamond, based on their performance) across the country, covering around ten locations a day. The earlier practice of soft loans was found to be less relevant, given the easy availability of cheap finance compared to the 1970s and '80s. EDDAL now supports funding of the service vehicle that mechanics use when going to attend complaints with a 10 per cent additional subsidy.

Dealers are happy that EDDAL is now active again, though they are slightly peeved that some services that were earlier provided free or at highly subsidised rates are now charged. Charges for training vary from fully paid to 50:50 sharing depending on the category of dealers, who have been divided into three groups. Nor are demo tractors available at subsidised rates. They feel this is a bit unfair as their contribution has been increased. But this is a minor grouse as they are quite happy with the overall cooperative approach of

Escorts. Dealer attrition more than halved from 10 per cent in 2017-18 to 4.2 per cent in 2018-19.

The approach to under-performing dealers has become more benevolent. Earlier, dealerships could be set up with as little as Rs 15 lakh, which was not a financially sustainable operation. Now, only those who can invest in a minimum volume of six tractors (which will mean an estimated investment of Rs 35 lakh) are appointed dealers. If the dealer is new to the business, then the Escorts sales team – from area manager to the field staff – extends all possible help to him. The dealer is given at least two years to stabilise his business. If, after two years, he is not found to be up to the mark, any decision on terminating his dealership has to be run past Nikhil Nanda, as he wants to be sure that the exit is for the right reason.

The changed approach to dealers also means Escorts had to invest a lot in re-orienting its own sales team. Sameer Tandon had found that the sales team was working with only dealers in mind. There was hardly any strategy to attract the end customers – the farmers. They had little clarity on why the farmer was buying a product and even competition was not defined. As a result, tractors were heavily discounted because dealers desired that, but the farmers were not buying tractors just because they were cheaper.

Tandon needed to work on the motivation levels of his field staff, as aggressive targets were being set for them to achieve. They were already low in morale and the coming of a new leader inevitably leads to apprehensions about being fired or sidelined. He needed to convince them that their fears were unfounded and that the company was going to invest in them. The HR department and Tandon worked closely to identify and encourage good performers and provide training avenues. Some people were fired but only on very obvious grounds like proven misdemeanour. Some of them had been thriving in a patronage-driven system and their exit sent out a message that good people would be protected and rewarded. As profitability started improving, thanks to cost rationalisation and quality enhancing initiatives like Project Shikhar, morale started to improve and the team began working in greater alignment.

ONE OF THE earliest moves towards becoming a friend of the farmer by listening to their requirements was the launching of the anti-lift tractor (ALT) in 2014. In the 2000s, there was a shift in the usage of the tractor to commercial operations like haulage. This required tractors to be faster as well as lug heavy loads, without breaking down. Other companies were quick to adapt and come up with products to tap into this market. Escorts, however, had remained content with catering only to farmers. When there were complaints about the tractors breaking down or lacking speed, the response was that tractors are meant to be used on farms. It was the change in focus after 2011, when Shenu Agarwal brought in a market orientation into R&D, that led to work being done on the ALT. Escorts's entry into the commercial segment was late, but at least it had now started to become more sensitive to customer demand.

Tractors, by themselves, do not mean very much beyond land preparation – they need various implements and equipments attached to be of value to the farmer. All tractor companies manufacture some implements, especially rotavators (which break up and aerate the soil and prepare it for sowing), but most of these are produced by specialised companies who may go by designs and specifications given by tractor manufacturers. As part of its goal of catering to all the needs of farmers, Escorts decided to get into the implements business itself, through a business vertical called SHIP set up in 2017. This would manufacture sprayers, harvesters, implements and planters (hence, SHIP). Apart from farmers, this initiative was also expected to help dealers, giving them an extra source of revenue, especially during the lean season for tractor sales.

SHIP set sail in 2018, focussing on implements already in the market – the rotavator and harvester. Another Faridabad-based company, Seitz Technologies India, was already manufacturing rotavators and it was decided that this would be brought into the Escorts brand and developed further through in-house R&D and partnerships. The rotavator has now been branded Escorts Farmpower (combining the names of Farmtrac and Powertrac). The production of the harvester, based on an Escorts design, has been outsourced to a Punjab-based company and is reported to be in huge demand. With these two, the SHIP division plans on becoming self-sufficient and then go all out to develop new products.

SHIP's R&D team, a small one of just eight young people in their twenties and thirties, goes to the field at least once a quarter, engaging with those who are directly or indirectly involved in farming, from farmers to mechanics to companies involved in agriculture-related activities. After identifying their pain points, the team starts working on designs of new products or tweaks to existing products.

There is a big focus on sprayers. Fields need to be sprayed with pesticides thrice in a cropping cycle and this is usually done manually with a can strapped on the back. This not only increases strain but is also hazardous. Attaching sprayers to tractors will take care of both these problems. Also on the anvil are specialised harvesters for paddy, potato and sugarcane, precision planters which are particularly important for paddy and a puddling rotavator. The common thread running through all these is to reduce drudgery for the farmer and increase productivity. SHIP had, till April 2019, done business of Rs 27 crore and has created micro-manufacturing plants with various collaborations. Business expansion will be planned in accordance with market demand.

Next it was the turn of the quality of service. After-sales service moved beyond repairing (though a lot was done to improve access to and quality of this) to giving customers a better experience. Dealers and Escorts Tractor Centre owners are being trained in how to interact with the customer and provide them various facilities, among other things. This has started to yield results. Escorts ranked last in a 2016 tractor service satisfaction survey of eight companies by market survey firm J.D. Power. In the 2018 survey, it had moved to fifth position and also logged the highest increase in the score.

Escorts is leveraging technology in a big way to improve customer experience. All tractors rolling off the assembly lines from 1 April 2019 have a device with a speaker phone, a SIM card and mike which will allow two-way communication between the farmer and Escorts round the clock. A farmer faced with a problem in his tractor can press this Care button and will, within minutes, get a call from a multi-lingual customer care centre, which will then connect him to an engineer. If the farmer's phone cannot be reached, then the engineer will speak to him over the device. If the problem cannot be solved online, then the query will be transferred to the nearest dealer, who will have to ensure that a service engineer or mechanic reaches the customer within two hours. The next part of Care's journey will go beyond solving problems that occur. Care Plus plans to help customers with preventive maintenance, alerting them about checks to be carried out and excessive variations in fuel consumption. Farmers with several tractors, some of which may be operated by others, can also keep track of their movement on their smartphones.

There will be little point in providing repair services within forty-eight hours if spare parts are not available. Escorts is now working on a plan that will eliminate the need for interventions of the kind HPN had to make – driving over 40 km from the outskirts of Delhi to Kashmiri Gate to solve the problem of spare parts an individual farmer was facing. Not only is it no longer feasible, given traffic conditions, it is also an inconvenience for the farmer. An initiative called Escorts Parts Eazy will have dealers connected with the company's spare parts division through a dedicated point of sale (POS) outlet. The dealer or his mechanic can then order whatever spare parts they need through this and have them delivered within shortest possible time. This will also protect the farmer from the thriving grey market for spare parts.

Realising that it was not easy for farmers to get loans for buying tractors, Escorts decided to get into the tractor financing space. In 2015, Escorts forged a tie-up with De Lage Landen (DLL) Financial Services India (the Indian arm of the DLL Group, a subsidiary of the Netherlands-based Rabobank) to provide retail loans with repayment options tweaked to suit the income cycles of customers. The actual operations, however, started a year later in 2016. Escorts Credit's portfolio size is now Rs 878 crore and it has funded the purchase of over 20,000 tractors across 490 dealers (64 per cent of Escorts dealers accounting for 72 per cent of overall sales. In 2018-19 alone, over 13,000 tractors were funded through Escorts Credit and the programme has been extended to self-propelled harvesters in Telangana, West Bengal and Chhattisgarh.

Attention has turned to moving beyond mechanisation.

FARM MECHANISATION IN India has a very low penetration rate, though it is an improvement over the situation two decades back. One of the reasons is that Indian agriculture is dominated by small and marginal farmers – 80 per cent of land holdings are below two hectares in size, which makes mechanisation at an individual level both unaffordable and unviable. Paradoxically, the attractiveness of mechanisation is growing, given that manual labour is both expensive and unreliable. Informal markets to rent out tractors and agricultural implements have always existed in villages and Nikhil Nanda started mulling over the idea of knitting this into an organised business, which could become a win-win for Escorts and the farmers. For him it was also about doing something for the community, something he had heard HPN speak of often. Around 2009, he started discussing the idea of farmers sharing various services which they could not afford individually with Mal and this led to Escorts venturing into the crop solution business in 2010.

When it started, Escorts limited itself to selling add-ons to tractors – planters, sprayers, harvesters, weeders – through the dealer network, which would then be rented out on an hourly basis. The business was muddling along when Sridhar introduced the idea of moving from selling products to providing farm mechanisation services. Getting the right business model was not easy and it took two more iterations before Escorts appeared to hit upon the right one.

The first model, launched in Odisha, was to sell paddy cultivation services with state-of-the-art equipment on a pay-per-use basis through dealers. Paddy cultivation was chosen for three reasons. One, being a large-acreage crop, paddy would make for better realisations. Two, it is a labour-intensive crop which made the case for mechanisation stronger. Three, this would give Escorts an entry point into the southern and eastern markets where its presence was still weak. Dealers were expected to invest in buying the required machinery – puddlers, planters, sprayers and harvesters – and provide end-to-end services, from creating nurseries to harvesting.

But the script went awry. Dealers needed to invest Rs 1 crore in getting all the machinery. No one was willing to put in such a large amount for a new business upfront; most put in only around Rs 25 lakh to get some of the equipment. Friction arose between dealers and farmers when the former were raising nurseries for the latter.

Farmers tended to be finicky when outsourcing operations and would often call dealers at odd hours, asking about, among other things, whether they had watered the nursery! If a nursery failed, the dealers had to bear the cost. In one case, where an Escorts team took up the work on behalf of a dealer in Vijaywada district of Andhra Pradesh, the farmer blamed them and demanded Rs 6 lakh as compensation, holding the equipment hostage till they complied. It turned out that the responsibility of watering the nursery was his and he had been remiss in this. It took a lot of negotiation and a reminder that the agreement said the liabilities would not be borne by Escorts for him to come around. Dealers, who are essentially traders, could not handle all this. There was the added problem of chasing farmers to pay for the services. Before long, dealers wanted out.

A consultant from an investment bank suggested trying the cooperative model, where a group of farmers would pool resources to invest in assets and Escorts would provide the services. It was felt that collections would be better in this model because the farmers, being locals, would be in a better position to identify who would pay and who would not. The responsibility was given to Nijagun Hiremath, who had been brought in from John Deere in 2010 to be part of the crop solutions team. Hiremath and his team of five decided on a limited liability partnership (LLP) model. Madan gave them some money and this model started with two LLPs in Odisha; later two more were started in what is now Telangana and one in Tamil Nadu.

Each LLP had five farmers who pitched in with Rs 50,000 each. The Rs 2.5 lakh investment was supposed to be the base to approach banks to finance the purchase of machinery. However, banks were reluctant, so Escorts decided to provide the machinery. There was enthusiasm initially and the LLPs got work orders, with some tractors doing more than sixteen hours of work a day at one point. Scaling up was on the cards and Hiremath had a target of twenty-five centres.

An assembly line in an Escorts plant manufacturing tractors

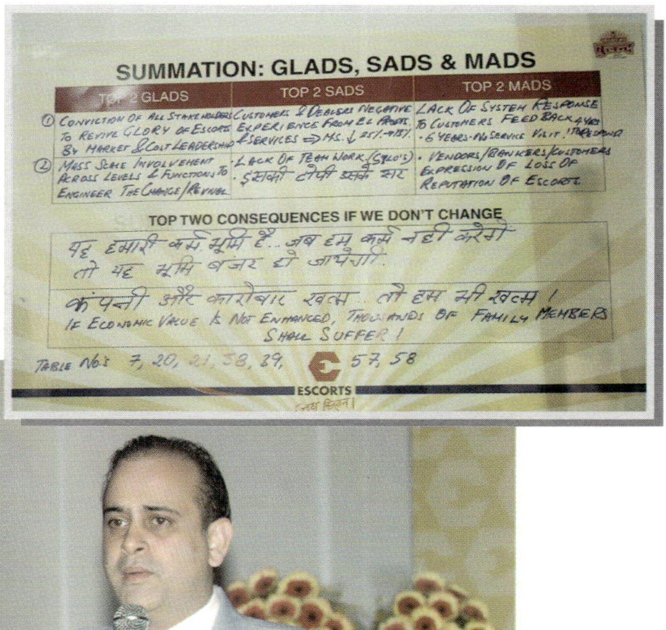

A large-scale interactive process (LSIP) session in progress

Nikhil Nanda and the senior Escorts leadership at a town-hall meeting with employees

Nikhil Nanda brainstorming with the R&D design team

Rajan and Nikhil Nanda meeting Escorts workers

Nikhil Nanda's town-hall meeting with employees

A town-hall meeting with young achievers

Nikhil Nanda signs the Escorts–Kubota joint venture with Masatoshi Kimata, the president of the Japanese corporation, in December 2018

Nikhil Nanda signs the Escorts–Tadano joint venture with Koichi Tadano, the president of the Japanese firm, in August 2018

RAJAN NANDA INNOVATION LAB
an Escorts initiative

The Disruptive Innovation Centre at the Escorts Knowledge Management Centre

A video grab from the Salman Khan-starrer *Sultan* (2016) featuring an Escorts tractor

Salman Khan in a TV commercial for *Sultan*, flanked by the Escorts Farmtrac and Powertrac tractors

A poster of *Jab Harry Met Sejal* (2017) featuring Shah Rukh Khan, Anushka Sharma and an Escorts tractor

The electric tractor developed by Escorts

Nikhil Nanda unveils the new hybrid tractor and a multi-utility rural transport vehicle at Esclusive 2019

India's first hybrid backhoe loader unveiled at Esclusive 2019

Unveiling the autonomous tractor
at Esclusive in August 2018

Unfortunately, the assumption that collections would be easier because of the familiarity of farmers with the customers of their services proved wrong. Just like providing services was not the core competency of dealers, collecting money was not the core competency of farmers. Ravi Menon, who was the CEO for a brief while after Sridhar's transfer to ECE, then suggested using specialised agents for recovery of dues. He pointed out that people who own harvesters provide these services in states far away from where they are located and never face a payments problem because they hire agents. Hiremath tried this out and found collections improved. He was asked to make a presentation on the experiment to board of directors member Hardeep Singh. Singh, with decades of experience in agriculture-related businesses, pointed out that the cash flow projections may go wrong and, if that happened, farmers would suffer and the Escorts brand equity would get hit. He suggested working on another model, but one where Escorts would not work on credit.

Hiremath was relieved at one level – most of his time had been taken up in the administrative task of setting up LLPs, leaving him little time to strategise. At another level, he was worried about the future of his team of seven on-roll employees. They then took off for the ETDC in Bengaluru and did some brainstorming. That led to a new model that is currently in operation.

In this, the Escorts Crop Solutions (ECS) unit (part of the agri-machinery division) brings together tractor owner-operators, farmers, agents and the ECS local team. Escorts markets the crop solution services, the agents convert enquiries into sales and ECS ensures that the tractor operators, who hitch Escorts implements to their vehicles, deliver services to the farmers. The agent pays Escorts in advance and the headache of collecting payments from farmers is entirely his. Hiremath pitched this to the management and Rs 20 crore was sanctioned for the project.

The new model was launched in August 2017 in Odisha, Andhra Pradesh and Tamil Nadu. The ECS team went about purchasing the necessary equipment, hiring agents and generating demand. They approached farmers, told them about the advantage of renting Escorts equipment and offered demos. There were initial hiccups – agents came on board but machines got delayed. Farmers were sceptical and had to be persuaded that Escorts was a sixty-year-old company that would stay and work for the long term. Harvester owners saw no reason why they should partner with Escorts. Finally, around 100 paddy farmers signed up for the service. ECS also provides plantation services – it has a polyhouse in the Yernagúda block of Rajahmundry district in Andhra Pradesh where paddy seedlings are grown in a controlled atmosphere.

Tying up with ECS has worked for both Rushi Keshav Rao and G.V. Ramesh, farmers in Yernaguda. Earlier both used local labour for puddling and transplanting of paddy, but good workers have become expensive and scarce. They tried using migrant labour, which is cheaper, but found the productivity and quality of machines much better. For example, optimum spacing between seedlings is not maintained when transplanting is done manually, while machines maintain the required distance. Farmers manage to plant six acres a day with machines – double of what manual labour covered. The cost of planting and growing is Rs 5,000 an acre when using labour; in the case of machines it comes down to Rs 4,500 an acre. The puddlers given by Escorts are also more efficient than the cage wheels farmers used. Seedlings grown in the polyhouse germinate in fifteen days and are ready for planting, while the seedlings grown in the customary way take twenty-five days to be ready for planting.

Providing the service has not been a cakewalk for ECS. It signed contracts with twenty-five harvester suppliers and gave a commitment to agents who had got orders. But on the day the harvesters were to reach, none showed up, even though the owners had been paid a handsome advance each. The agents who had taken money from farmers became abusive with ECS staff. Hiremath screamed and shouted but to no avail. ECS field staff had to hunt down the harvesters and forcibly bring them to the site but could find only thirteen of the twenty-five. Tractor and harvester operators continue to give ECS nervous moments. In 2017, five operators started making unreasonable demands regarding food and stay. ECS then had to pacify angry farmers. Every season requires a fresh search for operators, with no certainty that the same ones will return.

Collection continued to be a problem even under this model, except that this time the agents gave ECS the runaround. Hiremath then took the help of one of his managers who was from the telecom sector and quite aggressive in collections. He landed up at the agent's house at 3 a.m. and prepared to sleep there, saying money should be arranged by 11 a.m., when another person would arrive. The agent paid up. That incident sent out a clear signal to the market that ECS meant business and would not be fobbed off.

Between 2017 and 2019, ECS provided advanced mechanisation services to over 46,000 farmers, covering around 80,000 acres under paddy in Odisha, Andhra Pradesh, West Bengal, Tamil Nadu and Haryana. Importantly, it has generated business opportunities for more than 350 agri-entrepreneurs. The unit is now experimenting with encouraging local owner-operators. Just like ride-sharing taxi services like Ola and Uber that help finance the purchase of cabs which are then used on their platform, he has proposed to finance machines which will become the property of the operator after five years. The owner-operator will pay Rs 1 lakh per season to ECS, which will generate orders and handle collection, ensuring that he is paid for every hour that he works. In December 2018, twenty local people came on board to provide harvesting services to ECS. Not only does this create goodwill for Escorts in the local community and generate demand for its tractors and implements, but it also helps assure ECS of a dedicated supply of machines.

ECS has clocked Rs 7.68 crore revenue as of March 2019. It is not yet in the black, but it has become an important avenue for Escorts to connect with customers and give them a value proposition, apart from encouraging local entrepreneurship. As has another initiative which, fortunately, is less complicated.

AS OLA AND Uber disrupted the cab market in India's cities, discussion started within Escorts about replicating the business model for tractors. India has around 50 lakh tractors, most of which work for just about 400 hours a year (even accounting for commercial use like haulage) and remain idle the rest of the time. On the other hand, there are farmers who cannot afford tractors. The two needed to be matched up. That was also the case with implements; some are too expensive to buy for just one use in a crop season. But, as in the case of crop solutions, Escorts had to come up with a value proposition that would make this proposal more attractive than the existing village-level tractor and equipment renting businesses. That differentiator, it was decided, would be technology – farmers wanting to hire a tractor could use an app or call a toll-free number and get connected to a tractor owner; the call centre functions from 6.30 a.m. to 11 p.m. The initiative was named Traxi – a combination of tractor and taxi.

The Traxi division staff spent some months talking to farmers who owned tractors as well as those who hired them, in order to come up with a workable business model. The charge for renting the tractor and implements, it was decided, would be kept at 5 per cent below the prevailing market rate. But there was a condition – farmers hiring the tractors would have to pay the fee upfront against the usual practice of hiring on credit. Tractor owners liked this – getting 5 per cent less was more than made up for by upfront payments and an end to the hassle of chasing farmers for payments. For Escorts, the revenue comes from a registration-cum-annual fee of Rs 990 that it charges each tractor owner partner. In addition, it gets a commission of 3 per cent of earning from each assignment.

Traxi went live in April 2017 from the Mathura district of Uttar Pradesh, with fifty owners of Farmtrac or Powertrac tractors. The rent for the tractor is charged on an hourly basis or on acreage, with the rates varying from state to state or even in districts within a state. For farmers like Deepak, whose family grows potatoes on two bighas of land in the Nagla Rathi block of Mathura district, and Shiv Kumar, who grows potatoes and millets on 24 bighas of land in Fareh block of Agra district, Traxi has brought much relief. Earlier, tractor owners often made them run around for two or three days. Now they just call the toll-free number and are assured that the tractor and implements they need will come on time (a Traxi app has been launched but not all farmers own smart phones). Sometimes there are delays or no shows. In one case, the tractor owner who was also providing a potato digger cried off after completing four acres of a 50 acre contract. When such incidents occur, the Traxi field staff are quick to arrange for a substitute. Fortunately, such instances are rare. There have also been instances of farmers turning away a tractor they have called after it has reached. But tractor owners are not put to much loss or inconvenience because there is no dearth of demand during the crop season.

Traxi has meant an extra source of income for the tractor owners. Madan Lal, a farmer who earns around Rs 1.5 lakh through cultivating his 10 bighas of land, takes home an extra Rs 40,000 every season by renting out his tractor. He used to rent out his tractor even before Traxi entered the scene but he was wary about taking on customers because of the hassle of chasing them for payments. Because of Traxi's condition of upfront payment, he has taken on double the number of customers he used to earlier.

By 2019, Traxi has covered 3,000 villages in four districts of Uttar Pradesh, three in Haryana and one in Madhya Pradesh. Around 700 tractor owners are registered with it and close to 6,000 farmers have been hiring tractors and implements through it. Sixty per cent of the 4,500 farmers who used Traxi's services in Mathura district are repeat customers; Traxi has only been present for one season in the other districts, so whether or not there will be repeat customers will be known in subsequent seasons. Companies in the food processing business engaged in contract farming have also approached Traxi to help their farmers out.

Traxi has tough competition from other players in the market – organised players as well as the informal rental market. Realising this, it is now focussing on providing customer delight, so that it creates a market for Escorts tractors and implements. Right now, thirty-odd tractor owners have non-Escorts brands; they were taken on board so that Traxi could get an entry into their areas and the plan is to get them to convert into Escorts customers. Next, Traxi is planning to offer the rice transplanter that is part of the crop solutions portfolio to farmers in the rice-growing Karnal district of Haryana. It has already signed up 250 farmers for this and got advance payment of Rs 50 lakh for two months. The next plan is to provide harvesters also and take earnings to above Rs 1 crore.

TAKING CUSTOMER ENGAGEMENT a step further, Escorts decided to get into counselling for farmers on a range of issues related to agriculture. In early 2019, along with the introduction of the Digitrac tractor – a new brand of tractor with IOT (internet of things) features – Escorts launched the Digitrac app. Some of the e-commerce features in the app – booking a Digitrac tractor, applying for tractor financing and insurance – are available only in Punjab, where the first six tractors have been delivered. In the rest of India, farmers can download the app to get live weather updates, information on mandi prices and advice from experts on everything from what crop to sow to problems during the cultivation phase.

Many of these initiatives are still new. Some may not be very successful, some could be failures. For Nikhil Nanda, however, this is all about restoring the values of HPN in Escorts – that Escorts is more than a business, it is also about contributing to the community.

CHAPTER EIGHT

PARTNERING FOR PROGRESS

THERE IS NOTHING about the New Industrial Township (NIT) area of Faridabad to distinguish it from other industrial clusters in urban areas. The same narrow roads, with trucks being loaded or unloaded outside buildings behind high walls. The same hum or clackety-clack of machines inside those buildings. But this cluster, covering 742 sq km, was once the face of industrialisation and progress in Haryana, long, long before Gurgaon edged it out in the '80s. The township came up in the early '50s, when it was set up to rehabilitate Partition refugees from the area that is now Pakistan. They were given residential as well as factory plots to set up businesses. Some started supplying to Escorts, the creation of another victim of Partition, when the company first set up a factory in Faridabad in the '60s; others got into business because of Escorts. Among the latter were the units set up under the EEAL umbrella. In his memoir, *The Days of My Years,* HPN recalls one former chief minister of Haryana, the late Bhajan Lal, saying in the course of a speech: 'You can close any factory here, but you can't close this one. When you close Escorts you close 900 plants.'[1]

Some of these 900 were small companies like Yaman Industries, a supplier of hydraulic parts to Escorts. As a twenty-year-old, its founder, Tajinder Malik, had gone to deliver lunch to his father who was a worker at the Escorts railway equipment division. Impressed by the factory, Malik decided he would set up his own manufacturing unit. In 1982, he did just that, starting with one lathe unit and undertaking job work for NikiTasha, a cooking stove manufacturing company run by Ritu Nanda. Some years later, a Faridabad company supplying hydraulic parts to Escorts closed down and Malik quickly pitched for that business. His turnover then was Rs 3 lakh a month and he gives the entire credit to Escorts for Yaman Industries now having a turnover of Rs 1.3 crore a month. This relationship is not unique to Yaman Industries; most of the smaller suppliers, not just in Faridabad but in Delhi, Chandigarh and Punjab, have similar tales.

The large ones do too. Escorts was the second customer of Bharat Gears, founded by India's tyre industry icon Raunaq Singh, when it started operations in the mid-'70s in the Mumbra suburb of Thane, on the outskirts of Mumbai. Bharat Gears was Escorts's fourth supplier. In 2000, Bharat Gears's Faridabad factory was set up to cater only to Escorts, though it now supplies to other firms as well. When there was a strike at the Mumbra plant in 2001, Escorts sent its own people to keep the assembly line running. In 2009, when Bharat Gears approached Escorts for more business because its order book was almost blank because of the economic slowdown, Escorts gave it orders for transmission gears. And when in 2014 Bharat Gears wanted to move to a new dry cutting technology, Escorts was the only customer which supported it, though the company had approached others as well.

This close relationship between Escorts and its vendors suffered during the time the company was strapped for cash. Suppliers faced the brunt because their payments were among the first to be delayed, sometimes for six months at a time. A bill discounting system had been started in the late '90s, but this did not help beyond a point.

Many large companies, especially those which were single-source suppliers, tightened the screws on Escorts, refusing to supply till dues were cleared, though others like Faridabad-based Jai Bharat Maruti continued supplying, even though its dues climbed to Rs 2 crore. No one doubted Escorts's integrity but they would have had shareholders and boards of directors to answer to. Smaller companies did not have these institutional constraints and so had more flexibility. They, therefore, continued supplying. Malik of Yaman Industries took loans and squeezed his own suppliers as much as he could in order to keep his business going.

There was one positive fallout, however. As part of the efforts to get Escorts back on track, the payments system was streamlined. In 2008, strict deadlines were set for payments, and vendors started getting paid at regular intervals. And to put an end to corruption in the accounts department, payments were done through RTGS (real time gross settlement). This benefited all 800 firms supplying to the three businesses of Escorts, not just suppliers to the tractor division alone. In 2015, the tractor industry again witnessed a slump and payments had to be delayed. This time a letter, signed by Madan, went out in advance to all vendors, saying payments would be delayed by fifteen days. This was to help them plan their cash management. Ultimately, the delay was for just about a week. These actions helped Escorts win back the trust it had enjoyed with its suppliers. That was important because a turnaround of the company's fortunes would not be possible without bringing its suppliers on board. Indeed, once Escorts's fortunes started turning, vendors who had tied up with its competitors quickly returned to its fold.

THE BPR EXERCISE of the late-'90s was the first significant step Escorts had taken to modernise its manufacturing facilities. This was done by, first, improving the operational efficiencies of existing machines, from 65 per cent to 85 per cent. Where it was necessary, new machines were put in. As mentioned earlier, this not only increased the capacity to one lakh tractors from 72,000 but also led to plans of opening another factory near Pune being given up. But a few years after the BPR exercise was completed, it became obvious that a lot more needed to be done to raise the cost competitiveness of Escorts; improving the overall efficiency of the company's plants as well as that of its suppliers was necessary for this.

Around 2005, customer expectations in the tractor industry had started to change. From being satisfied if the tractor was sturdy and had a powerful engine, customers started getting finicky about fit and finish as well. Even if they were not of the kind Sridhar encountered in Varanasi – who kept a large tractor only for prestige – they were particular about the quality of paint and the sheet metal, as well as comfort and, most importantly, safety. This could not be done by limiting the focus to Escorts alone. Since bought-outs account for close to 98 per cent of Escorts production, it was necessary to pay attention to the production processes and quality in the factories of suppliers as well.

It was during Rohtash Mal's tenure from 2007 that the next step to improve overall competitiveness was taken. Of the fourteen projects that were taken up, supply chain transformation, material management and quality management were three. In collaboration with a leading consultancy firm, a fifteen-month programme was initiated which, when it ended, generated savings of 2 per cent a year on each tractor,[2] totalling to more than Rs 100 crore.[3]

This prepared Escorts for a bigger programme that was to follow five years later. After a benchmarking study commissioned by Sridhar showed Escorts trailing behind its competitors on a slew of parameters, a leading consulting firm was hired to help in a supplier excellence programme. The two-year project was named to reflect this goal – Shikhar, which means peak. The goal was to be the best in the industry in every facet of the supply chain. Launched in April 2014, Project Shikhar was led by two executives who had been key members of the BPR team – Shailendra Agrawal, who was then chief operating officer and head, R&D, of the agri-machinery division, and Ashok Gupta, then the head of quality, material and engine plant unit.[4] Over forty employees of the division were involved in the project, some of whom are considered rising stars in Escorts.

Shikhar had three elements – rationalising material cost, which was over 70 per cent of total cost, and bringing it on a par with the rest of the industry (66 per cent); reducing inventory from the prevailing seventeen days (against the industry benchmark of seven days); and rationalising the number of suppliers from 425 to 275.

The biggest success was achieved in material management, which ranges from market forecasting (forecasting demand for tractors) to supplier forecasting (how much raw material supplies would, therefore, be needed). An essential part of this is negotiating prices with suppliers on the basis of cost sheets drawn up by Escorts managers. It was not easy. The larger suppliers were particularly disinclined to bring down their prices. Escorts managers and executives benefited immensely from training in negotiation, which was part of the programme. The focus was on transparency and a spirit of give-and-take. Escorts managers learnt to research costs thoroughly and then confidently ask for fair reductions that protected the interests of both the company and its suppliers. At the end of two years, material costs had come down by 10 per cent, with no compromise whatsoever on quality or supply. Shikhar also helped in cutting raw material inventory, which came down to the industry benchmark of around ten days. Reducing raw material inventory by one day leads to a saving of around Rs 10 crore.

However, the targeted reduction in the number of suppliers did not happen. In fact, it increased to 500. That was the time Escorts was ramping up production and introducing new products, so not only did it need to keep existing vendors but it also had to get new ones who could supply components the earlier ones could not.

At the end of two years, Shikhar had not only brought down costs by Rs 185 crore, which was extremely significant for Escorts, but had other spin-offs like process improvements. The setting up of multi-functional teams also helped break bureaucratic walls between departments and fostered team spirit.

EVEN AS SHIKHAR was under way, Escorts had started to work closely with suppliers on quality. A supplier quality group was set up under the overall supervision of Shailendra Agrawal and Ashok Gupta (Sanjeev Mahajan took his place when he left). Headed by Ankur Gupta, head of quality management and plant engineering, the sixteen-member group first divided the 430 vendors Escorts had at that time into four quadrants, depending on their cost and quality:

- The elite club of fifty high-quality, high-cost suppliers, which were companies at par with Escorts.
- 310 high-quality, low-cost suppliers, whom those lower in the hierarchy should aspire to become.
- Fifty low-cost, low-quality suppliers who should try moving into the first two quadrants.
- Fifteen low-quality, high-cost suppliers who needed to be weeded out.

Companies in the first two quadrants undergo periodic random audits of processes, products and systems. If the Escorts team finds any gaps, action plans are worked out mutually. Companies in the first quadrant did not really need any handholding or mentoring by Escorts. However, many of them were monopoly suppliers and Escorts needed to do some de-risking by developing alternative suppliers for the components that they made. The memories of supplies being stopped by vendors during the financial crunch were still fresh in the minds of most people in Escorts. Having a second supplier was also one way of getting components at competitive prices by creating competition within and outside India. Wheel rims was one such component, where Escorts was at the mercy of a monopoly supplier. Escorts first got two Indian companies to provide wheel rims at more competitive rates and then sourced these from China as well. The former sole supplier's share of Escorts business has come down from 100 per cent to only 15 per cent. Every year now, before finalising contracts, Escorts takes a quotation from that company and the two negotiate prices. One year, the supplier agreed to a 10 per cent reduction in price for 20 per cent share in the business from Escorts. Over two years starting with 2017, ninety-one suppliers have been added in order to de-risk Escorts.

There is a lot of rigour now in the selection of new suppliers, with a cross-functional team doing a thorough audit spread over at least two days. The financial health of the company, its quality certifications and customer base are first scrutinised. Then the capacity and efficiency of its plant are checked, followed by an examination of its quality management system and process controls. Finally, the involvement of the top management is also studied.

The supplier quality group works very closely with the fifty low-cost, low-quality suppliers to help them become low-cost, high-quality suppliers. In the first phase, which started in 2014, twenty of these were chosen for mentoring. Escorts engineers and technicians visit their facilities and chalk out an improvement plan. They then visit the factories regularly and handhold them up to the implementation stage. After that, performance is monitored through fortnightly visits. In addition, engineers from the German certifying agency TUV are deployed at the facilities of both the high-quality, low-cost and low-cost, low-quality vendors. They not only check the supplies that these vendors send to Escorts, but also help the latter group with project planning and monitor their actions. Escorts has facilitated the tie-up of vendors with TUV, which also does the ISO certification for Escorts. Vendors have been made aware of the fact that the cost of these engineers is more than made up by improved profitability. In any case, since one TUV engineer looks after three suppliers, the individual cost is negligible. In 2017, fifteen more low-cost, low-quality suppliers were taken up for this mentoring, taking the count to thirty-five.

In 2015, Escorts expanded the TPM initiative it had started on its own shop floor to suppliers in the second and third quadrants. Thirty-six suppliers of critical components were selected on certain cost and quality parameters and trained in TPM to improve quality. Yaman Industries, one of the chosen few, was found to have a rejection rate of 5,000 ppm (parts per million) and was given a target of bringing it down to 2,000 ppm, which it did. There have been months in which the rejection rate has come down to 1,800 ppm. TPM started with one assembly line and has now been extended to all its lines. As a result, it has now bagged two large clients; once again Malik says it is all because of Escorts.

WHAT ALL CLASSES of vendors are particularly happy about is the change in the way Escorts interacts with them. Earlier, the relationship was transactional – Escorts would give orders for monthly or yearly supplies and vendors had no assurance about whether they would be supplying for the long term or for just a year or two. This transactional approach gave way to a strategic one in 2008. Annual conferences with 175 top suppliers were organised where they were told about the new products or product improvements that Escorts was planning. Later, Sridhar started interacting closely with the vendors, sharing both short-term plans and the Escorts vision for the future. The railway equipment division started the system of meetings with vendors, the first being organised in 2015. Nikhil Nanda shared Escorts Vision 2022 with vendors, which charts out the growth path for each of the three businesses. As a result, vendors can not only plan their production schedules for two or three years at a time but can also start thinking about investing in increasing their own capacities, something Malik is actively considering.

For Nikhil Nanda, the validation of the efforts that Escorts had made to restore the once-close relationship between the company and its vendor network came when he was on a flight to Bangkok in 2018. A man came up to him and introduced himself as a supplier of gears and shafts and said he enjoyed working with Escorts because of the fantastic energy and speed. 'But I also want to tell you,' he continued, 'that three years back I didn't want to supply to you because I had heard a lot of negative stories. Then I took a gamble and I am glad I did.'

For any original equipment manufacturer, the supplier is the backbone of the company. This is particularly true of companies which outsource the production of a majority of their components.

The cost, quality and timely delivery of the final product depends very heavily on the supplier. The relationship, therefore, has to be one based on trust and confidence. The revived Escorts certainly seems to have learnt that lesson.

CHAPTER NINE

ENERGISING THE EMPLOYEES

And the best news is that we are promoting all candidates internally from the company, and thus giving you all a chance to grow professionally and this is because your company acknowledges your hard work. Thank you, and I do firmly believe that we must invest into our people and you will see over time that we shall make a lot of investment in building our competence and together we shall grow on all fronts.

THESE WORDS ARE from a circular Nikhil Nanda put out on 14 February 2019, setting out an organisational restructuring of the top management – the first since he became chairman and managing director in August 2018 following his father's demise. Of the nearly dozen senior managers who had been elevated or given enhanced responsibilities, four had spent more than a decade with Escorts and stuck with it during its most difficult times. Both Shenu Agarwal, promoted to CEO of the agri-machinery division, and Rajneesh Agarwal, who had been made chief executive of FarmPower, had joined Escorts as graduate engineer trainees over two decades earlier and had remained there. Shailendra Agrawal, elevated as executive director of the group, had been with the company for over thirty years, though with a brief break in between.

It was important for Nikhil Nanda to send out this message. He had seen Escorts suffer in the mid-2000s as good executives left because they did not see a future for themselves in the company. He recognised that employees will give their best to a company when they see a career development path for themselves and when a company is able to feed their hunger for challenges. It was not that he was against bringing talent from outside; he certainly did not want Escorts to become an inward-looking company. Wherever necessary, the company would woo good people from other companies and, indeed, many named in the circular were less than five years old in Escorts. But unlike his father, whose first instinct was to look outside for talent, Nikhil preferred to first look inside. As he led Escorts on to newer paths, he knew building the morale of all employees – blue collar and white collar – was going to prove crucial for the journey. Fortunately, he did not have to deal with fractious industrial relations that his father had to.

THE NANDAS ARE typical large-hearted Punjabis and HPN was particularly so. This attitude carried over into Escorts's relationship with its employees and it had always been known as a generous employer. For HPN, employees – blue-collar workers or white-collar managers – were like family and needed to be treated well. Nobody was ever retrenched regardless of the company's financial position, and Escorts was, HPN writes in his memoir, the top paymaster of Faridabad. So, Escorts had largely been spared the strikes and lockouts that were an essential feature of the industrial landscape in the '70s and '80s, barring some minor incidents in Bengaluru and one in Faridabad in 1985. The latter one was resolved with give and take by both sides. The agreement brought in productivity-linked wages and stopped overtime but also ended the practice of hiring contract labour. Rajan Nanda continued with this magnanimous approach; he would often tell line managers that if the union was troublesome then it was a reflection on the management, which should introspect and correct itself.

That attitude worked in an era of limited competition, but had to change post liberalisation. Many companies did redefine the labour–capital relationship in the mid-'90s, but Escorts had continued with its large-hearted approach. In the late '90s, the tractor division had over 4,000 workers, far more than many of Escorts's competitors. With competitive pressures increasing, this was not going to be sustainable. The BPR exercise in the tractor division in the late '90s was an attempt to address this without retrenching workers. It was designed to increase both overall productivity as well as responsibility of individual workers and naturally sparked resentment. Rakesh Chopra and the BPR team led by Shailendra Agrawal had gone out of their way to communicate to workers and the union the benefits that the exercise would bring but to little avail. In December 1998, negotiations between the management and the All Escorts Employee Union (which was a common union for the whole group) on the three-yearly wage settlement broke down over productivity norms. That sparked a strike that lasted seventy days across plants in all businesses.

There was pressure on the management to give in to the union, since not just Escorts plants but factories of all suppliers in and around Faridabad were affected. But this time Rajan Nanda was persuaded to remain firm. When the management refused to blink – engineering trainees manned the lines and casual labour was hired, which led to some violence – the union came around. Some workers were sacked and a landmark agreement was signed in June 1999, under which the workers got handsome hikes in pay and allowances; one of them was that company buses would pick up and drop workers who commuted from nearby Haryana districts like Palwal and Hodal. In return, they had to agree to, among other things, multi-skilling and flexibility in being assigned work across machines and production stages, measurement of productivity by industrial engineering (IE) norms linked to output of machines and working hours, self-inspection and total productive maintenance (thus making them more accountable) and participation in quality circles. Apart from that there were conditions about punctuality, punching of cards, display of identity cards and misuse of office facilities for personal work.[1]

For its part, the management started communicating with the workers a bit more. The CEO (Chopra, at that time) would brief all levels of managers on the management vision and action plan.

The 1999 settlement did bring in a cultural transformation of sorts in Escorts, but it did not last long. As the tractor industry slowed down and competition increased, the management focus on discipline and productivity increased and this led to frequent flashpoints with the union, which was now headed by one of those who had had been dismissed after the 1998 strike, Bhupinder Singh (a person did not need to be an employee in order to become president of the union). In August 2001, Escorts was hit by another strike, sparked off ostensibly by an insect in one worker's food. The strike dragged on for eighty-four days. This time the management buckled under and some of those dismissed were reinstated, with retrospective effect. From then on, the management appeared to have lost the plot on industrial relations. Indiscipline on the shop floor started resurfacing. Managers were either not able or not empowered to take action against wrongdoers and disruptive elements. The top management did not want to do anything that would bring the assembly line to halt even for five minutes.

The company was in dire financial straits by the time the next wage settlement was due in 2003. Meanwhile, the management had worked on propping up more cooperative leaders. The union then agreed to a deferment of the wage settlement agreement till the company's financial position improved. In 2005, when the company's finances did improve with the sale of the hospital business, demands for a settlement started, accompanied by gate meetings and dharnas. After Ashok Chadha started ramping up production in the tractor division, it became impossible to delay the settlement any more. Simultaneously, efforts had been under way to sideline Singh and these were successful – he was dismissed for indiscipline with no adverse reaction from the workers – and the union elections threw up a more cooperative leader, S.D. Tyagi.

A settlement was inked in 2006 and the workers were happy with it, not just because of the raise of Rs 4,500 in the base salary, but also because it had a provision for jobs to children of workers who died when in service. The provision for employment to children of workers who died or retired had been introduced in the early '90s, but the number of such inductees was limited to a percentage of the workforce and a freeze was put on such hiring in 1994. Resuming this in the case of employees who died would not have been damaging by itself, but in 2007, when the company formulated a premature retirement scheme (for people who were not in good health), this provision was extended to their children. The idea was to compress costs – the more expensive older workers would be replaced by their children, who would get entry-level salaries. However, it affected productivity and discipline.

The Sankalp initiative that Rohtash Mal had organised went a long way in reforming union–management relations. When union leaders, who had a huge hold over the workers, went up on stage and vowed to do something, it had a cascading effect. Mal often used the pledges made at the Sankalp event to persuade the union to come around on various issues relating to discipline on the shop floor and improved productivity. Sometimes he just resorted to smart checkmating.

After the incident when he found empty liquor bottles in one of the manufacturing plants, he called a meeting of the union and spoke about the need for cleanliness. He then said his children often wanted to visit his office and that he was sure their children were also similarly curious. From the following Saturday, he said, workers could get their wives and children or other family members to the factory. He told R.K. Chilana to send circulars to workers' residences. The workers tended to live in clusters and the sight of someone from Escorts distributing letters created a buzz. In the plant the workers immediately got to work cleaning up their surroundings. The union just did not know how to counter this. Since then, every Saturday, around twenty families take a tour of the factory (in the course of which one woman remarked that the factory was cleaner than her kitchen), after which the plant head addresses them. They are then given lunch, which made some wives wonder why their husbands complain about the food in office! All this – and the customer visits that started in 2016 – led to workers taking pride in their surroundings.

One carrot, however, proved to be expensive. In 2010, the provision for employing children was extended to workers who retired in the normal course. Many of those inducted through this route were not the best fit for the job – some had only completed tenth standard and others, cocooned by the job security that Escorts offered, tended to be troublesome. So caveats started to be put in. In the 2013 settlement, this was limited to only those children who had finished twelfth standard. The 2016 settlement said only children of employees who had died while employed would be given jobs; the families were given the choice of taking employment or a lump sum of Rs 7 lakh.

Once Nikhil Nanda started getting more active in the business, he encouraged this carrot-and-stick approach. Like his father and grandfather before him, he believed that workers were part of the Escorts family and needed to be looked after. So he made sure the quality of food in the canteen improved, as did the air-conditioning facilities on the shop floor. He took the social engagement with the family further, with regular eye and health check-ups, blood donation camps and counselling for children who have just finished school. The annual Diwali function (a tradition continuing from HPN's days, complete with a bhangra performance by the workers) had an added feature – the children of some of the workers put up a performance too. The *World of Escorts,* a twenty-page quarterly company newsletter, with sections in Hindi, is sent to the families of all the workers. From 2019, an all-Hindi edition, *Escorts Pariwaar,* was started. This is meant to get workers and employees' families more involved with the company.

On the discipline front, Nikhil Nanda balanced firmness with fairness, unlike his father, who tended to be soft, often recommending pardon when the union appealed to him on behalf of a suspended worker. Nikhil empowered the line managers to take action against unruly elements and no appeals to the promoters were entertained. Union leaders could no longer assure suspended workers that they would be taken back with a meaningless apology or by threatening work stoppage. On one occasion, work was stopped after some workers were suspended for indiscipline. Union leaders appealed to various managers up to the level of Shailendra Agrawal, who was then group COO. They even tried going beyond him to the Nandas. But the message was clear: suspension will not be taken back without a proper enquiry, even if the assembly line does not move.

Other changes were ushered in to bring in discipline. If there was a production shortfall, whatever the reason, a no-production day was declared and workers given paid offs – only those who were required were called for duty. This decision was taken after the realisation that the indiscipline of the mid-2000s stemmed from workers idling around because of no production. Not only did this keep the workplace peaceful, it also helped in saving electricity and canteen costs. In the 2016 agreement, the system of allowing workers to take two hours off from their shift to attend to personal work was discontinued. Workers would invariably take a gate pass for two hours and then not return to their shift. A sweetener was thrown in that the office would try and help with whatever personal work the employee needed to attend to.

A four-member ER (employee relations) committee was set up comprising the group COO, head of ER, head of manufacturing operations and chief human resources officer (CHRO). This committee would deliberate on all demands not related to issues that were addressed in the three-yearly settlement.

With the change in the union leadership and the nuanced approach of the management, voluntary retirement schemes (VRS) to reduce manpower became smoother. The need to cut manpower became pressing when the benchmarking study commissioned in 2012 showed that Escorts's manpower costs were 10.5 per cent of sales, just short of double of many of its competitors. VRS had been an ongoing exercise for several years but now there was need to cut large numbers. So, in 2014, the terms were made more attractive. Those who still had up to three years of service left would get 100 per cent of their current salary while those with four or five years left would get 80 per cent. The internal target was to get 250 people to take VRS. Finally, 251 workers in the tractor division and another 49 in the auto product division took the offer. The overall reduction in the Escorts group as a whole was around 347. This VRS was what made the auto product division an attractive proposition for buyers. Escorts now has a permanent worker strength of around 1,700 across its three businesses; the tractor division is now down to 1,500. The deployment of contract workers has also increased to more than 50 per cent.

Communication between the management and workers has also increased. On the second Wednesday of every month, at the start of each shift, the plant head addresses the workers for ten minutes, telling them about the state of the company, the previous month's target and achievement of the plant and target for the following month. This is done at the same time across plants. Any worker who has contributed to quality or safety is honoured with a trophy. There was a plan for Nikhil Nanda to address them every three months, but this, unfortunately, has not happened. But high performers are labelled change agents and were invited to meet both chairman Rajan Nanda, when he was alive, and Nikhil Nanda.

The industrial relations scenario in Escorts in 2019 is a far cry from, say, a decade back. The workers now are more educated, they are actively involved in TPM activities, and women are present on the shop floor (a Nikhil Nanda initiative which has also helped improve the behaviour of their male colleagues). The 2016 settlement saw an increase in productivity norms and that did not set off any protests. Manpower costs have come down from 10.5 per cent in 2012 to 7.6 per cent in 2019. Above all, productivity has increased – since 2016-17, the tractor plants have been running close to their full capacity of 1 lakh tractors.

A similar change in culture was happening among the managerial staff as well.

WHEN ANIL KUMAR C., group head, HR, joined Escorts in September 2008 as general manager, HR, the first instruction he got was: 'You need to delay salaries by two days.' Two days' delay was actually an improvement; a year or two earlier, it was common for salaries of the managerial staff across hierarchies to be delayed for up to two weeks (salaries of the blue-collar staff had never been delayed) every month. It was no wonder, then, that he found employee morale low.

Low morale had not been an issue with Escorts at one time. It was a reputed group that paid well and figured among the top choices for employment by job seekers. The financial crisis had changed all that. Not only were salaries delayed, the quality of food in the canteen declined, electricity would be switched off at 5 p.m. and, worse, there was no putting up a brave face because the media had started writing negative stories about the company. Many had not left mainly because of the strong emotional bond they had with the company. A large number of employees lived in Faridabad and were often neighbours; they all thought of themselves as part of the Escorts family. Even work satisfaction levels had dropped. Escorts was not a very process-driven organisation and this both resulted in, and fed into, multiple silos headed by powerful individuals. The vicious and debilitating internal politics between them had a cascading effect on juniors in their departments. Anyone wanting to improve employee morale had to battle on multiple fronts.

It was necessary, first and foremost, to get cash into the system. Mal's SCORE initiative and the savings of more than Rs 100 crore that it generated brought a lot of relief. Next, Sankalp came and successfully shook the company out of the comfort zone it had slipped into. Having done that, Mal turned his attention to revamping the HR processes and identifying and nurturing talent within the organisation. Having worked in process-driven companies like Maruti Suzuki and Airtel, Mal wanted to bring their culture of focussing on employee development into Escorts. Indeed, he planted the seeds of a number of initiatives that were taken long after he had left. It was not easy either for him or Shalini Lal, an experienced HR professional, fresh from a PhD from the University of California Los Angeles, whom he brought in as CHRO. There was a clear division in Escorts between the traditional approach to HR which chairman Rajan Nanda favoured and the more modern approach that Nikhil Nanda was keen on. This division was something even Amanppreet Singh Bhatia felt when he joined as CHRO as late as 2017.

The culture clash became evident in one of Mal's early initiatives to start a 360-degree survey feedback for senior management – this feedback came from their seniors, peers and subordinates. This led to an uproar; managers wondered why subordinates should be asked to give a rating. It was explained to them that this was not a rating system, but more akin to holding up a mirror to them and they alone would see the report. It was accepted very grudgingly and only because it was seen to have Nikhil Nanda's firm backing.

Nikhil's first ask of Lal was to draw up a values statement for the company. This was important to give a sense of purpose and moral core to the organisation. In addition, it would give employees a better sense of what their company stood for and send out a signal to external stakeholders like customers, dealers and vendors that Escorts was not going to be an object of despair. Four core values – respect for people, empowerment, transparency and collaboration – and four strategic values – customer centricity, innovation, excellence and agility – were drawn up. Boards bearing these were put up all over the corporate office, as well as factories and outlets of dealers, apart from tent cards on the desks of employees. This, too, had been scoffed at by the older generation.

One big challenge that Mal and Lal faced was to change the outdated systems and processes in the company. As in the case of technology in tractor manufacturing, a lot of the initial work was really about catching up with the rest of the HR world. At a time when most companies had digitised HR systems and had fairly evolved Human Resources Information Systems (HRIS), Escorts was still relying heavily on paperwork. The annual performance assessments were the worst affected by this penchant for paper. The exercise would yield stacks of forms which no one had the bandwidth to go through and, as a result, ratings and increments were largely based on the whims and fancies of individual managers, who had probably made up their minds even before filling up the forms. There was no mid-year review or mechanism for feedback to employees.

In the new system, some of the criteria and weights that went into the overall score were changed, in line with what was happening elsewhere. The really significant development on this front was putting the performance management system (PMS) online. Increments were released on time for the first time the year this was introduced. But far more momentous was the fact that the transparency this entailed took away power from senior managers to indulge their personal biases. Given this, there should have been more resistance from the old guard. But some clever manoeuvring managed to avert this. The senior managers were not very familiar with these online processes and would ask for help from the HR department, which was readily given. Staff from the HR department would help with the keying in and operation of the online tool. By the time the ancien regime realised that the power and privilege of arbitrary decisions that they wielded had gone away, it was too late to stop the new process. Later in 2016, the PMS was refined, with key result areas (KRAs) being set, people being periodically assessed on these through the year and competency mapping done. The last had two elements – managerial competency across the organisation and functional competency; competencies had to be defined for each role and levels within that role.

In 2017, Bhatia further built on this, since individual KRAs did not necessarily align with what the company stood for or wanted. The need for setting the company's KRA, on the basis of which employee KRAs would be framed, was discussed at a general management committee (GMC, Nikhil Nanda and those reporting directly to him) meeting. An expert was called in to help and functional competency workshops with all the CEOs and senior management leaders were held, at the end of which the company's KRA was set. The expert pointed out that Escorts did not have a purpose line and that the motto, *Engineering the Fundamentals of Growth*, did not have an emotional connect. The purpose of each business needed to be set out, he said. The overall tag line then became 'Nation Matters' and within that each business got a purpose line. 'Powering the Dreams of Farmers' became the purpose of the agri-machinery business, 'Preferred Partner in National Development' was that of the construction equipment business and 'Ensuring Comfort and Safety in Indian Rail Transport' became that of the railway equipment division. The company's KRA then needed to be percolated to all the white-collar employees and the expert conducted several more sessions with 200 employees each. Following that, every employee's KRAs were aligned to that of the company.

Mal had also made the early efforts to build a competency framework in Escorts. He initiated the first assessment centre – a tool to measure management skills through a two-day event where people were put through psychometric tools, case studies and role plays. People who were in senior managerial positions were put through this and feedback was given on their capabilities and developmental needs. During Sridhar's time, this was built upon and a competency framework designed and formalised. People were assessed at three levels, representing upward career mobility: their ability to do their assigned tasks, their ability to build competencies of managing teams as they moved up the hierarchy and, finally, their ability to manage a business. Any training required was aligned to this.

Mal and Sridhar, between them, changed the way training was perceived in Escorts. When he joined, Anil Kumar C. had found that sending someone for training was a kind of punishment posting. Initially, small training programmes were designed to allay this fear. Soon a quarterly calendar of training was drawn up and lower- and middle-level managers regularly sent for these.

Succession planning was unheard of in Escorts and this was something Sridhar brought in. Nikhil Nanda, too, was keen on this. Potential leaders were identified through assessment centres and this time they were given rankings and feedback on how they fared as managers. Their past record in managerial roles was also taken into account and they were slotted as having high/low potential and as high/low performers. High performers with high potential were shoo-ins for top leadership positions. Sridhar and Lal worked out programmes akin to growth labs – addressing the mind, body and soul – that lasted a year to eighteen months for these managers. The first batch had people who are now in the top management like Shenu Agarwal or the next levels like Rajneesh Agarwal and, in 2019, a third batch was selected for this programme. Those who did not make the cut but still exhibited high potential were put through specific development programmes and had the managers they reported to having conversations with them on rising to their full potential – something that had never happened before in Escorts.

The assessment centres were not limited to the top leadership. When Sameer Tandon took charge as chief sales and marketing officer, it was decided to empower the sales team by enhancing their role. This meant identifying around forty territorial business managers out of 175 for promotion as area business managers and doing so in a way that was fair and seen to be so. That was quite a challenge. Tandon then decided the assessment centre was the best way to do this. Two-day centres were organised where external assessors put the sales team through the same exercise as for the top leadership, except that the case studies and role plays were designed to their specific context. Thanks to this exercise, one very energetic junior manager who was brimming with good ideas was promoted as a zonal sales head. Mid-level managers were put through an eighteen-month Programme for Accelerated Careers in Escorts (PACE), which used the methodology and assessment techniques of IBM Kenexa.

Identifying and grooming people for top positions was fine, but the question of whether they would stay after the company had invested time, money and effort in them loomed large. Once the company's financial position had improved, Mal got a compensation benchmarking survey done. Its findings were worrying. Escorts was at the twenty-seventh per centile in terms of salary, which meant that even mediocre companies were in a position to poach its managers. However, the financial position was still not robust enough to start giving handsome hikes across the board. Mal then devised a golden handcuff policy, wherein select people were promised hikes to be given at the end of specified periods that they stayed on for in Escorts. But there was also a need to keep the wage bill in check. It was around that time that the concept of variable pay – quite common in other organisations by then – was introduced in Escorts for certain levels and has now become widespread.

Recognising that annual salary hikes, increments or other incentives alone may not be enough, a rewards and recognition programme, Escorts Trailblazer, was started in 2019. Managers and team leaders are encouraged to give medals on the spot to an employee who may have done a great job. Those with the most medals become leaders of the month and the top three leaders get a meeting with Nikhil Nanda. In a parallel initiative, a Coffee with Nikhil programme was started, under which a group of six or seven high performers across departments get to chat with him. As part of the Trailblazer programme, senior managers are also given a kitty of immediate cash rewards, usually in the form of coupons, which they can give out to people reporting to them. The best team gets an annual CMD award. 'I appreciate' boards have also been put up in departments on which people can write about any colleague or someone else in the office; the person will then be given a certificate signed by Nikhil Nanda.

When Nikhil first met Sharad Gupta to interview him for handling the communications function, he had expressed his concern at the lack of internal communication. Indeed, what Gupta found was that one of the reasons for employee dissatisfaction at the middle and lower levels was seen to be a lack of connect with the organisation and the top leadership, especially Rajan and Nikhil Nanda. He got Nikhil to start town hall meetings with small groups of employees. Initially these were random, but over time this got institutionalised into two town halls a month, each with around thirty people. A virtual town hall, where the GMC takes questions from employees, was also started from June 2019. A monthly communiqué from Nikhil now goes out, telling people how the company is faring. A suggestion box is placed in every plant for people to drop notes and the box is opened by Nikhil himself.

HOW FAR HAS all this helped? In May 2017, Escorts participated, for the first time, in the Best Companies to Work For survey conducted by Great Places to Work and got a high score on the Trust Index. Earlier, wooing talent was difficult – good people were not interested in joining Escorts. That is no longer a problem and the group is able to get good candidates through campus recruitments.

Nikhil Nanda is a team player who has taken care to consult his top management team much more than his father did. By doing this, he has empowered that level and reduced scope for frustration. He has consciously tried to break the silos that were the bane of Escorts by creating GMCs and apex management committees (AMCom) where cross-departmental issues get thrashed out. But he himself readily admits that Escorts is still not a process-driven company and lacks adequate delegation of authority. This has the potential to diminish – if not actually nullify – the gains that his collaborative style and the various HR initiatives have brought in. He believes it will take another three years for Escorts to get to a recognisable level of process controls. Fortunately, the recognition of the problem – the first step to finding a solution – is very much there.

CHAPTER TEN

ALL SET FOR THE FUTURE

IN AUGUST 2018, Rajan Nanda passed away after a brief illness at the age of seventy-six. Close to sixty of those seventy-six years had revolved around Escorts – the last twenty-five at its helm. Even while he was in hospital, he would quiz Nikhil Nanda about office matters. He had seen its days of glory as well as its difficult times. But he did not die a sad or disappointed man. He was happy that Escorts had started to thrive again. He was particularly proud that much of this had happened under Nikhil's leadership.

From around 2013, when Nikhil became managing director, father and son had collaborated more closely than ever before and the points of tension between them had reduced significantly. They could not have disappeared entirely since they were two quite different – and strong – individuals. But they had forged a working relationship for the sake of what they were both passionate about – Escorts.

One of the last – and lasting – contributions that Rajan Nanda made to Escorts was to give it a board of directors that was far more value-enhancing than it was earlier.

A revamped Companies Act, enacted in 2013, required a restructuring of the boards of directors of companies from 1 April

2014. The Act had stipulations relating to, among other things, the role of promoter chairmen, appointment of independent directors and rotation of non-independent directors. The restructuring in many companies was just an exercise in formality, merely adhering to the letter of the law. Rajan Nanda, on the other hand, acknowledged that the board had to be packed with talent if the company had to be taken to the next level. He decided to use this opportunity to do so.

The new Act's provisions meant that the number of directors on the Escorts board had to increase from six to ten. Rajan Nanda gave careful thought to the selection of each director and what that person could bring to the table. One woman director was mandatory, but Rajan Nanda made sure he got the best – Vibha Paul Rishi, a seasoned marketing professional who had also made significant contributions in the HR field. P.H. Ravikumar brought a finance perspective, Hardeep Singh (who had been a member of the earlier board) an unparalleled experience in agri-related businesses, Sutanu Behuria his experience in the bureaucracy and D.J. Kakalia his legal acumen. G.B. Mathur was inducted because he was part of the Escorts legacy and had been involved in various restructurings the company had gone through and Nitasha Nanda because she had been involved with various subsidiary companies. Sunil Kant Munjal of the Hero group is the latest inductee in 2019 in place of one member who had to step down.

Rajan Nanda did not stop at packing the board with talented people. He sought to ensure that the board played a more active role than before in advising and giving strategic direction to the company. Dates for meetings are fixed a year in advance and communicated to the directors. If they are not able to be physically present, they join in through video conference, thus ensuring full attendance at all meetings. Annual operating plans are discussed with the board and debated at length. The net result of all this is not only that Escorts now has expert advice available on tap but there is greater trust between the management and the independent directors.

For Nikhil, having such a board as he took over as chairman after his father's demise was a godsend. The responsibility of nurturing Escorts, giving it a vision, direction and sense of purpose, was now on him along with his team under the board's guidance.

In 2017, Escorts had framed Vision 2022. This envisaged a two and a half times growth in revenue in five years, EBIDTA touching 13-14 per cent, return on capital employed of around 30 per cent and exports accounting for 10 per cent of its turnover. Beyond these dry numbers, the vision was also about imbuing the company with a larger purpose. HPN used to read newspapers to get a sense of what the nation needed; 'Nation Matters' is the core of the Escorts that Nikhil is now steering.

Nation Matters is about eliminating drudgery from the life of Indian farmers by providing them affordable, high-quality products. It is about contributing to Indian infrastructure with cutting-edge technology. It is about leveraging Indian frugal engineering and marrying it with the best of global technology to be tapped through strong partnerships. The resolve to make life easier for farmers is not about technology alone, but new platforms as well, like rental and shared services in the form of Traxi and Escorts Crop Solutions.

TUCKED AWAY IN a corner of the verdant corporate headquarters of Escorts is an E-shaped building, known as the Knowledge Management Centre (KMC). One room in that building has fun written all over it. The first sight that greets a visitor to the Disruptive Innovation Cell is a set of drums and a guitar propped up against the white wall, the floor is carpeted with artificial grass, some seating is in the form of faux wooden logs, and a cane balcony swing seat with a bright orange cushion hangs from the ceiling. Ten-odd work stations are scattered around, with young people hard at work.

A larger group of around twenty, known as the technology platform team, is busy in another larger room on the same floor, drawing and re-drawing engine designs or doing complicated calculations on their computers. This room is staid in comparison, barring an orange bean bag and a table tennis board breaking the monotony of a normal open office.

The appearance and ambience of the two rooms may be quite different, but the 350-odd young men and women working in them are the key to the technological excellence that Escorts is striving for. Innovation is becoming a key differentiator at the company, with 6 September being observed as Innovation Day since 2017, the highlight being Esclusive (combination of Escorts and exclusive), an event that showcases the unique technologies developed by the company's engineers. The outlay for R&D, which used to be just around 1 per cent of turnover at one time is now over 2 per cent.

The technology platform team is working on the third layer of the technology roadmap that Sridhar had drawn up – future most advanced. This is all about new products that are at the cutting edge of technology. The Disruptive Innovation Cell, as the name suggests, was set up in end-2017 to work on the fourth layer – disruption and innovation – to come up with unique, futuristic concepts in the tractor industry. The technology platform group has a brainstorming meeting every Friday where ideas and suggestions from the team itself, the Escorts leadership as well as the market are discussed. The brief to the team from the top management is short and sweet: focus on the customer and come up with ideas that will make the tractor owner's life easier and happier.

The first heady moment for the entire KMC team was the unveiling of the concept of the world's first compact electric tractor[1] at the first

Esclusive in 2017. Escorts's 22 HP electric tractor is suitable for, among others, vineyards and orchards, has zero emissions and can be charged through ordinary power sockets at home. Work on rolling it out has been going on since then – getting customer feedback, soft launches in Europe, the United States and India – and Escorts is planning to launch it in the European and American markets by 2020. For the Indian market, issues like charging the battery have still to be dealt with.

The following year, a concept autonomous tractor was unveiled. This is not going to be a driver-less tractor, but will automate close to 80 per cent of operations. With the help of geo-fencing,[2] tractors can move in a straight line and turn automatically when they reach the boundaries of a field being ploughed, without the turns either overlapping an already ploughed area or leaving wide gaps. It will also improve precision in sowing operations, leading to higher productivity, apart from reducing farmer fatigue. This was developed with seven global technology majors, some of them long-standing partners like AVL and several first-time partners like Silicon Valley-based navigation systems developer Trimble, vehicle control systems maker WABCO (which originated as part of the Westinghouse group) and Microsoft. The team in Escorts is now working on the tractor's interface with the various implements that get attached to it.

Alongside, Escorts launched India's first hybrid tractor, which will use both conventional fuel and electricity. In the 90 HP tractor, the power for 75 HP will be through the engine and the rest through electricity, which will mean much lower emissions than the conventional tractors. It will also enable the farmer to switch seamlessly between electric and conventional power whenever the situation demands.

In addition, it launched India's first backhoe for smart construction equipment technology. And, working on the urban–rural connect and addressing the issue of mobility for hard rural terrain and ploughing functions, the company has also worked on and showcased the concept of India's first multi-utility rural transport vehicle (RTV), which will help farmers in both transport and logistics, in addition to providing earning opportunities from haulage and commercial transport.

Rajan Nanda had always been interested in finding tech solutions to all the problems farmers faced. In a fitting tribute to him, before Rajan Nanda Innovation Lab (RNIL) has been set up. Taking disruptive innovation beyond mechanisation, serious effort is being put into addressing a host of other issues, from water management to soil conditions to weather, that have a bearing on farmers' productivity and profitability. Located in what was his office area, it will work closely with academia and tech companies in India and abroad to incubate innovative technology solutions relating to soil nutrition, reducing wastage and storage.

RNIL, headed by Sharad Gupta, is also exploring tie-ups with agro tech and start-up companies in Israel, Australia and the Netherlands. Collaborations are planned with the Indian Institute of Technology (IIT), Bombay, on projects related to clay mineral fertiliser, seeds storage system, water management sensors, among others, as also with IIT Delhi on methane-based alternative fuel. RNIL is no esoteric indulgence to remember Rajan Nanda by, exploring impractical ideas. Sharad Gupta and chief technology officer Ashwani Malik, who heads KMC, will be working closely to study how the solutions that RNIL throws up can be integrated with the work KMC is doing and the larger agri-business portfolio.

WANTING TO BECOME a company driven by innovation and with aspirations of becoming a global player has its own set of organisational challenges. The organisation needs to be lean and mean, with financial flab giving way to financial muscle. More importantly in the case of Escorts, governance systems and processes needed to be toned up to make the organisation more nimble and less bureaucratic. Escorts got the best consultants to work alongside it on all this.

The Rs 185 crore savings on just material costs from Shikhar had made Escorts realise that cost management was something it needed to give serious attention to. Around 2016, it again hired a leading consultancy firm to study the cost structure. Potential points of saving were identified across the organisation and Project LEAP (Let's Engage And Perform) was launched in 2017. It had four objectives, to be achieved over three years: to bring down fixed costs to 8-9 per cent of revenues, accelerate sales of tractors to get to 15 per cent market share domestically, grow revenues from spare parts to more than 10 per cent of total revenues and enhance contribution by the backend (materials cost, backend and the like) by 10 per cent. Each cost centre was assigned one person from the consultancy firm who worked closely with the leaders to achieve these objectives.

A lot of investment and effort went into toning up the human resource systems, for both blue-collar and white-collar employees, as the previous chapter showed. The bar for performance of the company was also raised. Earlier, Escorts had been benchmarking itself with competitors on quality parameters on its own. In 2016, it decided to participate in annual surveys by J.D. Power, the global consumer ratings company. Similarly, the system of internal auditors was done away with. Instead, the task was handed over to a professional audit firm, first Grant Thornton and later EY, which would give their report to the chairman and thereafter to the audit committee of the board of directors. Escorts also upped its game on a slew of corporate governance measures. It adopted a Code of Business Conduct, reaffirming the company's adherence to various corporate laws, a Whistleblower Protection Policy, a dividend distribution policy committing the company to distributing up to 20 per cent of profits as dividend to shareholders and a code of conduct on insider trading which makes it mandatory for those above the rank of chief general manager with access to information on strategic developments in the company to inform the company about any trading they do. The company also put in place a policy on preserving email records for a specified number of years and another one on sexual harassment, detailing processes to be followed in case of any complaint. These were all important signals coming out of Escorts that it was going to be a more process-driven company than it was before.

Nikhil was acutely conscious of the fact that an organisation would deliver the best only when power and decision-making did not get over-centralised and senior managers were empowered. Rajan Nanda had taken the first steps to professionalizing the management of Escorts but had not been able or willing to step back entirely. It was a paradoxical situation where he would both give his senior management immense freedom and also breathe down their necks.

On the other hand, even when he was managing director, Nikhil had been putting in place systems and processes that would cut through the silos in the company and reduce bureaucratic red tape as well as his own hands-on involvement in day-to-day management. Regular meetings of the group management committee (comprising the chairman and managing director, CFO and all CEOs) and flash meetings (financial overview by the GMC and functional heads) ensure that the organisation as a whole is more aligned to a common goal. Communication between various levels is almost instantaneous; there are several WhatsApp groups and Nikhil is part of all the important ones. The days of waiting to get an appointment with the CMD and then waiting for his response are over.

Nikhil had been clear even before he became chairman that he would move completely out of an operational role at the right time. He felt that time had now come. That was what the management restructuring of February 2019 was designed to do.

By creating the post of an executive director whom all the CEOs of the three businesses would directly report to, Nikhil set the stage for eventually moving into the role of mentor-guide. The executive director – Shailendra Agrawal was named as the first – would be responsible for the group's overall operating performance and strategic growth. Six years earlier, Nikhil would probably have had reservations about Shailendra. He had been part of the select circle around Rajan Nanda, some of whom Nikhil had not been comfortable with. But the various talent spotting and development initiatives had thrown up his name repeatedly and Nikhil decided to put the organisation above his personal biases. Over time both men developed an equation based on trust and soon Nikhil began to increasingly see Shailendra as the right person to head the group. The final deciding factor was his role in the negotiations with Kubota, which he led after Sridhar's exit; the second most powerful man in Kubota, Kitao, told Shailendra, in front of Nikhil: 'Mr Agrawal, you negotiated well.'

Apart from the executive director, the only other person reporting directly to Nikhil is Bharat Madan, the group CFO, who would have a dotted-line reporting to the executive director. Madan was also designated corporate head, which makes him responsible for alignment of individual businesses with corporate functions as well as group financial management. This is to ensure that there is greater alignment of objectives within the group, something that had not been there at all.

Having handed over the operational baton to Shailendra Agrawal, Nikhil has decided to concentrate on the larger picture and chart new courses for Escorts to embark on, stepping in only when it was absolutely necessary. Even as managing director, his style was more collaborative and enabling. He gave a broad direction to his managers and the confidence that they would have his unstinting support so long as they were working to bring about transformation in the company. Some six months before the restructuring, he had stopped attending AMComs and confined himself to GMCs and flash meetings.

With the latest move, he hoped to carve out more time for networking on behalf of Escorts and engaging with the policy establishment and business chambers, something he had not got the time for earlier. One of the first things he did once the new management structure kicked in was to go on a fifteen-day trip to the United States accompanied by the board of directors for meetings with investment funds and talking to reputed research organisations for possible collaborations for RNIL.

In taking this step, Nikhil has become the latest business dynast to decisively move in the direction of separating ownership from day-to-day management. Other family businesses have professionalized in fits and starts – taking one step forward and two steps back – but groups like Eicher, Dabur and Murugappa have gone beyond cosmetics to meaningfully distance the family from operational control. Escorts is on its way to joining that league.

MOST DAYS, AFTER lunch in his office, Nikhil sits on a grey sofa in an ante chamber and stares at three frames on the wall. One is a picture of his grandfather. It serves as a constant reminder of Escorts's storied legacy and the need to restore that and the values his grandfather epitomised. The other two are charts which show where Escorts's main rivals are positioned on various parameters. They show him the ground Escorts still needs to cover.

Reflecting on Escorts's past may just give him pointers for the group's future.

What made Escorts one of the icons of Indian industry? Undoubtedly, it was the ability of HPN to spot business opportunities in things the country lacked. It was among the first few companies to launch tractors at a time when a wooden plough driven by a pair of bullocks was the defining face of Indian agriculture. Along with Rajan Nanda, he then built it up into a diversified engineering company, ranging from auto components to construction equipment and two-wheelers. The latter captured the imagination of both rural and urban youth in the 1970s and 1980s; Rajdoot motorcycles gave a rural-terrain biking experience and the Yamaha an urban biking experience.

There was also the desire to give the best to the customer. Hence the stellar partnerships that Escorts forged – with Ford, JCB, Yamaha, Goetze, Hughes Telecom. It was not just about the best in technology, but equally about the best in service. HPN's way of connecting with customers and other stakeholders holds valuable lessons even today, fifty years later. When Escorts lost this touch, after he stepped back into retirement, it took quite a few knocks. Nikhil Nanda is now bringing those values back. The collaborations with the Japanese – Kubota in tractors and Tadano in construction equipment – will, he hopes, not just give Escorts a global footprint but give its employees exposure to process excellence and quality focus. The form of connecting with customers and stakeholders may be different, but he is bringing back the old spirit.

What made Escorts flounder? The history of the company also holds lessons on how businesses need to be agile, nimbly navigating changes in the policy environment and market place. The opening up of the economy in 1991 brought new opportunities for Indian businesses but also increased competition. Escorts lacked this agility. Rajan Nanda was certainly quick to tap into new business opportunities that liberalisation threw up, notably telecom and healthcare. So did other manufacturing companies. But the competitive landscape was not something he managed very well. Escorts succeeded in healthcare as much because competition was limited – Apollo Hospitals was the only other corporate hospital chain of significance – because of the nurturing that Rajan Nanda provided. However, he was less successful in growing the far more competitive and cash-guzzling telecom business. There are both generic and particular reasons for this. In part, this reflected a dyed-in-the-wool manufacturing company's inability to make the mindset switch that the services sector required. After all, the Aditya Birla group's Idea is the only example of an old-economy company making a success out of its telecom foray. Specifically, Escorts did not have the deep pockets that the telecom business required. Bringing in another investor could have helped but Rajan Nanda's steadfast reluctance to dilute was an insurmountable hurdle.

Unfortunately, Escorts did not also successfully navigate the competitive landscape in its main business of tractors. Post 1991, with the coming of global biggies like John Deere and New Holland, Mahindra and TAFE were quick to realise that the tractor market was a volumes game and snapped up companies that had tractors in HP ranges they did not have. They managed to get a national footprint even as Escorts did not move beyond the northern and western markets. Escorts did try to penetrate the southern market, which was where growth was happening, but these efforts were feeble at best.

That organisational agility is far more important today given the pace of technological change and the disruptions they bring in their wake is one lesson that Nikhil Nanda seems to have internalised. Hence the current Escorts emphasis on disruption and innovation, across businesses. Hence also the collaborations with leading technology players in the design and rollout of new products.

Having steered Escorts out of choppy waters, Nikhil wants Escorts to consolidate the gains and build on them. He is confident that the Vision 2022 goal of market leadership is within touching distance. Along with his top management team, he is now drawing up a Vision 2027, which is about Escorts extending its ambitions to beyond the country's borders. The prospect of taking Escorts back to the days when it was a diversified group is tempting, but, for now, he is sticking to the knitting – tractors, construction equipment and railway equipment. There are immense opportunities to be leveraged in just these three areas, given a favourable policy environment in the form of increased government focus on agriculture and infrastructure. The shares of the construction equipment and railway equipment businesses need to be increased in order to protect the group from the vagaries of the tractor business, whose fortunes swing with those of the rainfall-dependent Indian agriculture. He is also mulling over blue ocean diversifications aligned to Vision 2027 that include exploring inorganic growth opportunities. He is trying to create an Escorts where people come to work with a sense of purpose – about making an impact on society at large. And, above all, he is trying to create an institution whose future will not be dependent on the fortunes of one family, an institution that can outlast the Nandas, if it comes to that. He is sure his grandfather is watching with approval.

NOTES

Chapter one: The Journey Begins

1. This chapter is drawn largely from H.P. Nanda's memoir, *The Days of My Years* (New Delhi: Penguin Books, 1992).
2. 'A Case Study of Restructuring at an Indian Organization: Escorts Auto Components Limited', http://shodhganga.inflibnet.ac.in/jspui/bitstream/10603/202690/16/16_chapter7.pdf.

Chapter two: Fashioning a New Escorts

1. The hotel is now known as The Oberoi and the 360 restaurant is located where Versailles–La Rochelle used to be.

2. Dilip Bobb, 'I have been criticised all the way: Rajan Nanda', *India Today*, 31 March 1981, https://www.indiatoday.in/magazine/cover-story/story/19810331-i-have-been-critised-all-the-way-rajan-nanda-772779-2013-11-25.

Chapter three: The Swing into Services

1. 'Escotel Cuts Long-Distance Rates in UP', *Business Standard*, 16 December 1997, https://www.business-standard.com/article/specials/escotel-cuts-long-distance-rates-in-up-197121601060_1.html.
2. Chairman's message, Annual Report 1999-2000.
3. Sanjay Anand, 'Escorts closes telecom deal with IFC', *The Times of India*, 15 August 2002, https://timesofindia.indiatimes.com/business/india-business/Escorts-closes-telecom-deal-with-IFC/articleshow/19109506.cms.
4. In 2007, Hutchison Essar was sold to Vodafone.
5. Annual Report, 2003-04, p. 7.
6. H.P. Nanda, *The Days of My Years* (New Delhi: Penguin Books, 1992).
7. Ibid.
8. 'Escorts Heart due diligence still on, says Merlion', *The Hindu Business Line*, 6 August 2003, https://www.thehindubusinessline.com/2003/08/06/stories/2003080601680300.htm.
9. Annual Report, 2005-06, p. 47.

Chapter four: Slipping into Coma

1. BIFR was a quasi-judicial body set up in 1987 under the Sick Industrial Companies (Special Provisions) Act, 1985. The board of directors of any company whose net worth had got eroded

had to compulsorily refer it to BIFR and attempt to work out a revival/closure plan.

2. Bhupesh Bhandari, 'Escorts: Fending off hostile takeover, surviving family split', *Business Standard*, 6 August 2018, http://www.business-standard.com/article/companies/40-years-ago-and-now-escorts-fending-off-a-hostile-takeover-and-surviving-a-family-split-114110500008_1.html.

Chapter six: Powering Ahead

1. An ancient Chinese military treatise considered to be authored largely by military strategist Sun Tzu. Its lessons have often been applied to businesses.
2. Pininfarina was acquired by the Mahindra group in 2015.
3. 'Press Release: Escorts Introduces indigenously engineered Electric Tractor at Agritechnica 2017, Hanover, Germany', http://www.moneycontrol.com/stocks/reports/escorts-press-release-media-release-9908761.html.
4. Annual Report, 2015-16.
5. This was a take-off on a line that Tata Steel used – we also make steel.

Chapter eight: Partnering for Progress

1. This could have been a reference to the suppliers of all the businesses Escorts was in during HPN's time or the entire chain of suppliers, that is, suppliers to suppliers of Escorts.
2. *The Shikhar Times*, 30 April 2015.
3. Nikhil Nanda quoted by Shally Seth and Baiju Kalesh in 'Escorts takes to the tractor again' in *Mint*, 19 August 2010, https://www.

livemint.com/Companies/T4kY6Sr5jzIqDfiIzBsaaP/Escorts-takes-to-the-tractor-again.html.

4. Ashok Gupta has since left Escorts.

CHAPTER NINE: ENERGISING THE EMPLOYEES

1. Arun Kumar and N. Meenakshi, 'A Declining Market Mars a Historic Collective Bargaining Agreement: The Case of Escorts', *Vikalp*, Vol. 31, No. 2 (April-June 2006).

CHAPTER TEN: ALL SET FOR THE FUTURE

1. The only other electric tractor is from the German firm Fendt, and is a larger 67 HP one.
2. GPS or RFID technology is used to create virtual geographical boundaries which will be linked to appliances.

INDEX

GLOSSARY OF ABBREVIATIONS

AGNI	A short-range ballistic missile developed by the Defence Research and Development Organization
ALT	Anti Lift Tractor
AVL	AVL India Pvt Limited
BCS	BCS Italy
BIFR	Board for Industrial and Financial Reconstruction
BPL	BPL Limited
BPR	Business Process Re-engineering
CEO	Chief Executive Officer
CFO	Chief Financial Officer
CHRO	Chief Human Resource Officer
CKD	Complete Knock-down
CMD	Chairman and Managing Director
COO	Chief Operating Officer

CRM	Customer Relationship Management
DCM	Delhi Cloth Mills
DSE	Dealer Sales Executive
EACL	ECO Auto Components Limited
EAM	Escorts Agri Machinery
EAP	Escorts Auto Products
EBIDTA	Earning Before Interest Depreciation, Tax and Amortization
EBIT	Earning Before Interest and Tax
ECE	Escorts Construction Equipment
ECEL	Escorts Construction Equipment Limited
ECS	Escorts Crop Solutions
ED	Executive Director
EDDAL	Escorts Dealers Development Association Limited
EEAL	Escorts Employees Anciliaries Limited
EHIRC	Escorts Heart Institute and Research Centre
ER	Employee Relations
ERP	Escorts Railway Products
ESMS	Escorts Sales Management Software
ETDC	Escorts Training and Development Centre
ETL	Escorts Tractors Limited
FNA	Farmtrac North America LLC
GE	General Electric
GMC	Group Management Committee
HP	Horse Power
HPN	Hari Parshad Nanda
HR	Human Relations
HRIS	Human Resource Information System
IBM	IBM India
ICC	International Chamber of Commerce
IED	Industrial Equipment Division
IIT	Indian Institute of Technology
IOT	Internet of Things
IR	Industrial Relations
IT	Information Technology

ITI	Industrial Training Institute
JCB	J.C. Bamford Excavators Limited
KMC	Knowledge Management Centre
LG	LG Corporation
LLP	Limited Liability Partnership
LS	LS Mtron Limited
MIS	Management Information System
MSD	Motor Cycle Division
NRI	Non Resident Indian
OEM	Original Equipment Manufacturers
PABX	Private Automatic Branch Exchange
PhD	Doctor of Philosophy
Plant 1	EAM Plant 1
PMS	Performance Management System
QIP	Qualified Institutional Placement
R&D	Research and Development
RED	Railway Equipment Division
SHIP	Sprayers, harvesters, implementers, planters
TAFE	Tractor and Farm Equipment Limited
TPM	Total Productivity Managament
TRAI	Telecom Regulatory Authority of India
VRS	Voluntry Retirement Scheme
WABCO	WABCO India Limited

ACKNOWLEDGEMENTS

TRACKING HISTORY, WHETHER the hoary past or current, is always a challenge. It is not adequate to rely on records alone. Dry facts need to be brought to life with anecdotal accounts and vivid memories. We faced one major setback soon after we started working on this book – the passing away of Rajan Nanda. Fortunately, we were able to track and talk to many executives who had worked closely with him in shaping Escorts – Umesh Banerji, Rakesh Chopra, Rajan Swaroop, M.M. Mehta, Manoj Kohli, N.K. Pandey, G.B Mathur. Their accounts helped us piece together Rajan Nanda's tenure and his approach to business and management. Their contribution to this book has been enormous because Nikhil Nanda too was unaware of the many facts they helped uncover.

Nikhil was generous with his time and recollections. In addition, many other former Escortians helped us put together the story of how Escorts was slowly pulled back from the edge of the precipice. They played key roles in this turnaround and we thank Rohtash Mal, Shailendra Tandon, Sameer Tandon, S. Sridhar and Shalini Lal for sharing their perspectives. The current top leadership of Escorts – Shailendra Agrawal, Bharat Madan, Shenu Agarwal, Ajay Sharma, Dipankar Ghosh and Ajay Mandahr – added enormously to the accounts of these stalwarts.

Ritu Nanda and Shweta Bachchan Nanda helped bring out the human aspects of Rajan and Nikhil Nanda, with Ritu Nanda particularly providing a useful perspective on the generational shifts in approach between HP, Rajan and Nikhil Nanda.

Nijagun Hiremath, Ashwani Malik and Rajneesh Agarwal were kind enough to share details of the businesses they are heading. The chapter on employee relations would not have been possible without Amanppreet Singh, Anil K.C., B.S. Dagar and Imteyaz Ahmed; the chapter on vendors without the perspective and details shared by Ashok Gupta; and the chapter on customers and marketing without the inputs of V.K. Puri, S.P. Pandey and dealers Seema Gupta, Bimal Agarwal and his son Vinamra Agarwal.

We thank Nimesh Kampani and Rakesh Jhunjhunwala for sparing time for us from their busy schedules. A special word of thanks for Adi Godrej, who acceded to our request for writing the Foreword.

And finally a shout-out to Vicky Chauhan, Prateek Singhal and Nidhi Sharma of Escorts.

We don't think we have left any names out. In case we have, we seek forgiveness – the omission is purely inadvertent.

ABOUT THE AUTHORS

SEETHA is a senior journalist with thirty-five years of varied experience – from covering the Babri Masjid demolition to tracking economic policy. She is the author of *The Backroom Brigade: How a Few Intrepid Entrepreneurs Brought the World to India* and co-author, along with R.C. Bhargava, of *The Maruti Story: How a Public Sector Company Put India on Wheels*.

SHARAD GUPTA is Chief Communications Officer, Corporate Marketing & Brand Strategy, and Vice President, Technology Innovations, at Escorts Limited. He has been with the organization since 2014 and witnessed its recent turnaround from close quarters. He has authored a number of articles for business publications and other media platforms.